Discovering

BLACK
NEW YORK

Discovering BLACK NEW YORK

A GUIDE TO THE CITY'S MOST IMPORTANT AFRICAN AMERICAN LANDMARKS, RESTAURANTS, MUSEUMS, HISTORICAL SITES, AND MORE

TEXT AND PHOTOGRAPHS BY
LINDA TARRANT-REID

CITADEL PRESS
Kensington Publishing Corp.
www.kensingtonbooks.com

CITADEL PRESS books are published by

Kensington Publishing Corp.
850 Third Avenue
New York, NY 10022

All Kensington titles, imprints, and distributed lines are available at special quantity discounts for bulk purchases for sales promotions, premiums, fund raising, educational, or institutional use. Special book excerpts or customized printings can also be created to fit specific needs. For details, write or phone the office of the Kensington special sales manager: Kensington Publishing Corp., 850 Third Avenue, New York, NY 10022, attn: Special Sales Department, phone 1-800-221-2647.

Citadel Press and the Citadel logo are trademarks of Kensington Publishing Corp.

First printing July 2001

10 9 8 7 6 5 4 3 2 1

Printed in the United States of America

Library of Congress Control Number: 2001092651

ISBN 0-8065-2144-9

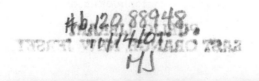

CONTENTS

ACKNOWLEDGMENTS

I want to thank everyone who has been so generous and kind to me during this project, especially my agent Marie Brown, my editor Carrie Cantor, photographer Marvin Smith, Elizabeth Wells of Wells Supper Club, Donald Bogle, Deborah Walker, Angela Iadavaia-Cox, Juanita Dawson-Rhodes, Sandy Parker, Glenda Johnson, Heywood Dotson, Khadijah Matin, John Crow of the Langston Hughes Library, Bessie Edwards of New York City's African American Ethnic Heritage Task Force, James Huffman of the Schomburg Center for Research in Black Culture, Dr. Sherill D. Wilson and Libby Jackson of the African Burial Ground Project, Tony Thomas, Dr. Robert Swan, Roger Martin of the Queensborough President's Office, Jim Driscoll of the Queens Historical Society, Anna French of Historic Weeksville, Julia Shaw, Peter Ostrander of the Kingsbridge Historical Society, Sylvia D'Alessandro of the Sandy Ground Historical Society, Muriel Sumama of Harlem Spirituals, Inc., Amy Herling of Macomea Design, Anthony Bowman of A La Carte New York Tours, Inc., Fred Laverpool of Braggin' About Brooklyn, Phil Davis, Darryl T. Downing, Gwen Hankin, Doug Frazier, Cynthia Reid, Gale Colden, Gwen Byrd, Joan Pina, Wendy Nelson, Traci Jones, Leslie Mostyn, and especially my husband, Stuart Reid, and my kids, Gibby and Siad.

PREFACE

"New York, New York, the Big Apple," intoned Harlem's spoken-word rebels, the Last Poets, in their 1960s rhyme about the huge metropolis. "So nice they named it twice," was another familiar chant that expressed the awe and excitement many had for New York City. The Big Apple is a nickname given to this bustling city by the black jazz musicians who flocked to New York City in the 1920s to get a slice of the work that was abundant during the Jazz Age.

New York City is, indeed, every one of those things and more. The poems, the rhymes, and the jazzy renditions celebrating the City in all of its many incarnations are marvelous advertisements for the wonderful experiences that await the visitor. Diversity is the hallmark of the City. Immigrants from all over the world have been greeted since 1886 by the Lady in the Harbor with her torch hoisted high, beckoning new arrivals to, "Give us your tired, your poor, your huddled masses, yearning to be free." Bringing their culture and their traditions, these immigrants come ashore to make a new life.

However, not all of the immigrants debarking from ships in the harbor looked forward to their new homeland. There were some who came from Africa as indentured servants, and others who came as slaves. This is their story.

In America's colonial days Africans were brought to this small island as indentured servants or, as some historians have written, as slaves to clear the land for the settlers of the Dutch West India Company. Later, enslaved Africans were transported from their homelands in shackles to work in New Amsterdam (as Manhattan was then called), first under the Dutch and then under the British. *Discovering Black New York* traces the steps of these first Africans as they gained their freedom, purchased land, and established their own institutions.

The guide takes visitors on a journey to the Five Points District in lower Manhattan, the first neighborhood blacks settled after slavery was abolished in 1827 in New York State; to the free black settlements of Seneca Village, Weeksville, and Sandy Ground; to the Little Africa section of Greenwich Village and the black neighborhoods of the infamous Tenderloin and San Juan Hill sections; and finally, to Harlem and the outer boroughs.

Much of the early history of black New York has been erased, but the recent discovery of the eighteenth-century African Burial Ground, formerly known as the Negroes Burial Ground, is a poignant reminder to all that there are many secrets beneath the concrete and steel. The 20,000 graves at this forgotten site were uncovered by a bulldozer making way for another skyscraper— they might have been lost forever if it had not been for a group of dedicated individuals who forced the government to halt construction. New York City bears witness to this undiscovered history in the many unmarked sites where freed blacks attended school, conducted business, and established their own churches, as well as the designated landmarks and cultural venues that celebrate the contributions of black people.

Discovering Black New York begins with a short history and then, borough by borough, provides listings of historic sites and landmarks, museums and galleries, restaurants, clubs, shopping, and tours. Manhattan, Brooklyn, Queens, the Bronx, and Staten Island each have a unique story of their earliest African residents.

My hope is that you will sit back and take it all in, and, at some point, with *Discovering Black New York* in hand, explore the wealth of history of black Americans in New York City up close. I also hope you will visit my Website at www.blackny.com for the latest information on black New York.

To Juanita Edith and Marcus Hannah
And with all my love
To Stuart, Siad, and Gibwa

Discovering
BLACK
NEW YORK

INTRODUCTION

African Americans in New York City

EARLY HISTORY

According to documented history, the first blacks to arrive in Manhattan (which was then called New Amsterdam) were eleven Africans brought over in 1626 by the Dutch West India Company to clear the land and build forts, roads, and houses in the Dutch colony of New Netherland, which stretched from the Delaware River near present-day Burlington, New Jersey, to Albany, New York. The Dutch West India Company, a trading company created by a group of Dutch merchants, was chartered in 1621 to develop commercial trade opportunities and establish settlements to support their business in the Americas and West Africa. The Africans came over as "company negroes" and are referred to in various historical accounts as indentured servants and slaves. Among the names listed in company records were Anthony Portuguese, Paul D'Angola, Simon Congo, Jan (John) Francisco, and Peter San Tomee. Their surnames, it is believed, indicated the homelands these men left behind. Several years later three African women were imported to New Amsterdam.

The rush to colonize New York started after the explorer Henry Hudson visited these shores in 1609. Henry Hudson set sail from the Netherlands on his ship, the *Half Moon,* looking for a shortcut to the Orient to increase trade for the merchant-owners of the Dutch East India Company, the precursor to the Dutch West India Company. Hudson and his crew embarked on this journey following a northeast course, only to be turned back by the ice-clogged waters off the coast of Norway. Undaunted, Hudson changed direction and sailed west. On this course, the *Half Moon* eventually reached North America. The *Half Moon* followed the coast south, past Maine, Massachusetts, Virginia, and then the ship traveled north up the Delaware Bay, finally reaching the mouth of the river that became Hudson's namesake.

Henry Hudson was not the first European explorer to reach the Hudson River. In 1524 Italian explorer Giovanni Verrazzano sailed to the mouth of the Hudson searching for a similar shortcut to the Orient for King Francis I of France. Unable to navigate the Narrows, the snug passageway between Brooklyn and Staten Island, and faced with an unexpected storm, Verrazzano turned back. Around 1525 Portuguese explorer Esteban Gomez followed that same westerly route sponsored by Spain's King Charles, but, he, too, turned back after only reaching the Upper Bay, not far from Governor's Island.

As early as the sixteenth century, Europeans explored northern New York and developed trade relations with Native Americans. And it is believed that around 1540, French traders traveled down the river from the north to what is now Albany to trade with the Wappingers and the Mohicans. Shortly after Hudson's voyage in 1614, Henrich Christiansen and Adrien Block headed expeditions sponsored by Dutch merchants to exploit trading opportunities with the Native Americans. Christiansen and his group sailed up the Hudson River to Albany and built a trading post, which was named Fort Nassau. Adrien Block explored the lower Hudson Bay and named the waters on the east side of Manhattan Island Hell's

Gate. He then sailed north toward Cape Cod and encountered an island off the Connecticut coast, which he named Block Island.

The Dutch West India Company had established the colony of New Netherland in 1624 under the direction of Cornelius Jacobsen May. The first settlers were thirty families of French-speaking Huguenot protestants and Walloons, who had escaped religious persecution in France and were living in the Netherlands. Eight men settled on Governor's Island in the East River, eighteen families traveled north to Albany near where Fort Nassau stood and established Fort Orange, and the others settled on the Delaware and Connecticut Rivers. This was the beginning of twenty years of Dutch colonization in the New World.

Willem Verhulst became director of New Netherland in 1626 and moved the settlements on the Delaware and Connecticut Rivers and the Governor's Island settlement to Manhattan Island. At around the same time, Manhattan Island was purchased from the Native Americans for the equivalent of 60 guilders. Some historians credit Verhulst, and others his successor, Peter Minuit, with the purchase.

During Peter Minuit's term as director, a fort was built in lower Manhattan, and the settlement was named New Amsterdam. By the 1640s, New Netherland was the largest importer of African slaves, and by 1654 New Amsterdam was the center of the Dutch slave trade. The slaves worked as farmers, laborers, and craftsmen. The expense of slavery soon became burdensome and the Dutch instituted a policy of "half-freedom" that allowed slaves the freedom to pursue their own lives when they were not working for their masters. Under the Dutch, Africans could petition the courts in legal matters, own property, marry, and, in some cases, be baptized.

In 1644, eleven blacks petitioned the courts for their freedom. Among the eleven were Anthony Portuguese, Jan Francisco, Simon Congo, Paul D'Angola, Peter San Tomee, Big Manuel, and Little Manuel. They were among the original group of enslaved men brought to the colony in 1626. The Dutch granted the men and their wives conditional freedom, but not their children. The freed Africans were given land, which included a two-mile stretch from Canal Street to 34th Street, and taxed twenty-two and a half bushels of corn, wheat, peas, or beans and one hog to be given to the Dutch West India Company each year. In the event that they defaulted on the agreement, they would be returned to slavery. One of the earliest recorded black landowners was Catelina Anthony, a freed African woman who owned eight acres in what is now known as Chinatown in 1643.

In 1653 Governor Peter Stuyvesant had the slaves build a wall around lower Manhattan to fortify the island against the threat of attack. The street near the wall became known as Wall Street. However, the wall was not a factor during the British takeover, as Stuyvesant surrendered to Colonel Richard Nicolls after a bloodless coup by the British on September 8, 1664. After the British takeover, New Amsterdam was renamed New York, in honor of the Duke of York who was gifted the land by his brother King Charles II of Britain. The population of New York was then approximately 1,500, and the population of the colony of New Netherland was 8,000, including 700 blacks.

With the arrival of the British, slavery became a regulated business, and the importation of African and Caribbean slaves increased dramatically. By the early 1700s, there were more than 3,000 slaves in the colony. By 1711 the Market House at the Wall Street Slip was established as the principal market where blacks and Indians were sold as slaves, and whites were sold as indentured servants.

The first organized slave rebellion, known as the Maiden Lane Incident, occurred in 1712. About thirty blacks set fires to buildings in the center of town, and attacked and killed whites who attempted to put out the fires. After the British captured and executed the slaves thought to be responsible for the insurrection, they avenged the riots by enacting repressive laws, called the Black Codes, including one that prohibited blacks, Indians, and mulat-

City of New-York, *ſs.*

A LAW

For Regulating Negroes and Slaves in the Night Time.

BE It Ordained by the Mayor, Recorder, Aldermen and Aſſiſtants of the City of New-York, convened in Common-Council, and it is hereby Ordained by the Authority of the ſame, That from hence-forth no Negro, Mulatto or Indian Slave, above the Age of Fourteen Years, do preſume to be or appear in any of the Streets of this City, on the South-ſide of the Freſh-Water, in the Night time, above an hour after Sun-ſet; And that if any ſuch Negro, Mulatto or Indian Slave or Slaves, as aforeſaid, ſhall be found in any of the Streets of this City, or in any other Place, on the South ſide of the Freſh-Water, in the Night-time, above one hour after Sun-ſet, without a Lanthorn and lighted Candle in it, ſo as the light thereof may be plainly ſeen (and not in company with his, her or their Maſter or Miſtreſs, or ſome White Perſon or White Servant belonging to the Family whoſe Slave he or ſhe is, or in whoſe Service he or ſhe then are) That then and in ſuch caſe it ſhall and may be lawful for any of his Majeſty's Subjects within the ſaid City to apprehend ſuch Slave or Slaves, not having ſuch Lanthorn and Candle, and forth-with carry him, her or them before the Mayor or Recorder, or any one of the Aldermen of the ſaid City (if at a ſeaſonable hour) and if at an unſeaſonable hour, to the Watch-houſe, thereto be confined until the next Morning) who are hereby authorized, upon Proof of the Offence, to commit ſuch Slave or Slaves to the common Goal, for ſuch his, her or their Contempt, and there to remain until the Maſter, Miſtreſs or Owner of every ſuch Slave or Slaves, ſhall pay to the Perſon or Perſons who apprehended and committed every ſuch Slave or Slaves, the Sum of Four Shillings current Money of New-York, for his, her or their pains and Trouble therein, with Reaſonable Charges of Proſecution.

And be it further Ordained by the Authority aforeſaid, That every Slave or Slaves that ſhall be convicted of the Offence aforeſaid, before he, ſhe or they be diſcharged out of Cuſtody, ſhall be Whipped at the Publick Whipping-Poſt (not exceeding Forty Laſhes) if deſired by the Maſter or Owner of ſuch Slave or Slaves.

Provided always, and it is the intent hereof, That if two or more Slaves (Not exceeding the Number of Three) be together in any lawful Employ or Labour for the Service of their Maſter or Miſtreſs (and not otherwiſe) and only one of them have and carry ſuch Lanthorn with a lighted Candle therein, the other Slaves in ſuch Compay not carrying a Lanthorn and lighted Candle, ſhall not be conſtrued and intended to be within the meaning and Penalty of this Law, any thing in this Law contained to the contrary hereof in any wiſe notwithſtanding. Dated at the City-Hall this Two and Twentieth Day of April, in the fourth year of His Majeſty's Reign, Annoq; Domini 1731.

By Order of Common Council,

Will. Sharpas, Cl.

Legislation regarding the restrictions on Negroes and slaves at night. April 22, 1731. This law was part of the Black Codes, a series of laws that prohibited blacks from congregating in groups for fear they were planning revolts. (From the Photographs and Prints Division, Schomburg Center for Research in Black Culture, The New York Public Library, Astor, Lenox, and Tilden Foundations) toes from owning and inheriting land. The laws also discouraged the freeing of slaves—a common practice under the Dutch—by requiring ex-slaveowners to pay 200 pounds a year for life to the freed slave.

As of March 1741 white fear had heightened as rumors of a Great Negro Plot circulated. After a series of fires were set, a white indentured servant named Mary Burton accused a number of slaves and a white tavern owner and his wife of a plot to burn the entire city and murder white citizens. Chaos ruled, and by the time it was all over, more than 150 slaves and twenty-five whites were arrested. Eighteen blacks and four whites were hanged, thirteen slaves were burned at the stake, and seventy slaves were deported.

A significant number of blacks also lived in Brooklyn, which was settled by the Dutch in 1635. Jan Francisco, one of the original Africans imported to the colony by the Dutch West India Company in 1626, became a founder of Bushwick (Boswyck) in 1661. The census of 1698 recorded 296 slaves out of a total population of 2,017, and by 1738 King's County was the leading slave-holding county in New York. In 1790 blacks were more than one third of the population, with 1,482 slaves and only forty-six free blacks. These figures contrasted greatly to the 1,036 free blacks in Manhattan at the same time.

During the Revolutionary War (1776–1783) many Africans fought on both sides. The British originally hired enslaved blacks as laborers, and in the fall of 1775 they paid them to help fight the war. General George Washington followed suit in January 1776. Blacks fought battles at Bunker Hill, Saratoga, and White Plains. James Brown, a black man, was an aide to General Washington during the war. (Brown is pictured in the oil painting of *Washington Crossing the Delaware* by Emanuel Leutze that hangs in the Metropolitan Museum of Art.) When the British were defeated in 1783, more than 3,000 freed and enslaved Africans who had fought during the war migrated to Canada; others sailed to Great Britain.

Slavery was abolished in New York State in 1827, although a gradual decline in the sordid institution began around the late 1700s. More and more runaway slaves fled to New York City and free blacks migrated to this thriving community and opened businesses, purchased land, and established organizations such as schools, mutual aid societies, and churches to support and service the burgeoning black population. In 1787 the African Free Schools were established to educate black children by the mostly white New York Manumission Society (founded by Alexander Hamilton and John Jay, among others). Two of the Society's earliest schools were located at 245 William Street and 137 Mulberry Street. The African Free Schools became part of the New York Public School Society in 1834. The New York African Society for Mutual Relief was founded in 1808 and chartered in 1810 by Peter Williams Sr. and others to provide financial aid to its members and their families. Peter Williams was also a co-founder of the Zion Church (1796) on Church and Leonard Streets, the oldest black Methodist church in New York State. Today, Mother A.M.E. Zion Church is located in Harlem. (See page 73.)

An important business located in lower Manhattan during this period was owned by Thomas Downing. He migrated from Chincoteague, Virginia, in 1819 and opened Downing's Oyster House at the corner of Broad and Wall Streets. By the 1830s, Downing's Oyster House had become famous for serving the city's politicians and other prominent individuals, including British novelist Charles Dickens. Downing also sent his famous oysters to Queen Victoria who, in appreciation, gifted him with a gold chronometer. He and his son George helped hide fugitive slaves in the cellar of their restaurant.

After slavery was abolished, many blacks moved to the Five Points District in lower Manhattan, where they lived among poor Irish immigrants. According to the 1830 census, 14,000 blacks lived in Manhattan. The black section of Five Points was called Stagg Town or Negro Plantations. The dilapidated tenement buildings, houses of prostitution, and saloons were a sleazy backdrop to the rampant disease, extreme poverty, and criminal activity that was part of daily life.

Several community organizations formed to aid the black population in New York. Mary Murray and Anna Shotwell created a home and school for black children when they opened the Colored Orphan Asylum at 12th Street and Sixth Avenue in 1836. The Association for the Improvement of the Condition of the Poor built the Workingmen's Home in 1855 to house poor blacks at Mott and Elizabeth Streets.

As the black population attempted to assimilate into the community, tensions increased between freed blacks and whites competing for jobs and decent housing; eventually, this tension erupted into race riots. During the Draft Riots of 1863, the Colored Orphan Asylum, which was then located on Fifth Avenue between 43rd and 44th Streets, was set on fire by a mob angry about being drafted to fight in the Civil War while wealthy citizens bought exemptions from the draft. The mobs roamed the streets of New York and beat, killed, and burned blacks and destroyed their property. The riots, which resulted in 105 deaths, were the bloodiest urban disturbance in U.S. history at the time.

Black residents of the Five Points District had begun their exodus to Bleecker, Sullivan, Wooster, Thompson, MacDougal, and Carmine Streets in Greenwich Village by the 1830s. In the 1890s, movement continued as blacks searched for better housing, and took up residence on the West Side between 40th and 50th Streets, the area then known as the Tenderloin, but more recently called Hell's Kitchen. They also moved to San Juan Hill in the West 60s (currently the site of Lincoln Center), a neighborhood settled by German and Irish immigrants. San Juan Hill, it is said, earned its nickname because of the many black veterans who settled there after returning from the Spanish-American War. These poverty-stricken communities were filled with overcrowded tenements and rampant crime. Tensions between blacks and whites were high and street brawls occurred regularly. The San Juan Hill neighborhood was the center of black life in New York City in the early twentieth century.

At the end of the nineteenth century, black churches, businesses, and organizations also moved to midtown locations creating a large and vibrant community. Seventh Avenue from the 20s to the 40s was known as African Broadway. In 1900 the Marshall, a hotel on West 53rd Street, became a center of black cultural life. Actors, musicians, singers, dancers, and composers socialized at this seat of entertainment in "Black Bohemia." The hotel was home to poet Paul Laurence Dunbar, composer Will Marion Cook, and writer Bob Cole.

The black press emerged in New York after slavery was abolished, to fill the information void that the newly freed experienced. The first black-owned newspaper in the United States, *Freedom's Journal*, was started by John Russwurm and Reverend Samuel Cornish in 1827. The paper advocated abolition and equal rights for blacks. It ceased publication in 1829. David Ruggles, a free black from Connecticut, published the *Mirror of Liberty*, another antislavery newspaper, from 1838 to 1841. He also opened the first black bookstore in 1834 at 67 Lispenard Street; the store was used as a reading room for blacks who were not allowed in the public library. An abolitionist, Ruggles was a founder of the New York Vigilance Committee that protected free blacks from being kidnapped into slavery. He also published the *Slaveholders Directory*, a listing of the names and addresses of politicians, lawyers, and police in New York who participated in the kidnapping of free blacks. Ruggles's home at 36 Lispenard was used as a station on the Underground Railroad. The *New York Age*, one of these post-abolition newspapers, began publication in 1884 as the *New York Freeman*, with T. Thomas Fortune as publisher.

THE TWENTIETH CENTURY

By the turn of the century, black New Yorkers were involved in all facets of city life. In what became known as the Great Migration thousands of blacks moved from the South and the Caribbean to New York City seeking a better life. Black political power became a factor in New York's political landscape. Black Republican Charles W. Anderson was appointed chief of New York State Treasury in 1914, and in 1916 a black man was appointed to the New York City Council. Harvard graduate Ferdinand Morton, the leader of the United Colored Democrats, was appointed civil service commissioner for delivering the black vote in the election of 1917 in which John Hylan became mayor.

Along with the Great Migration there arose a so-called Great Debate between Booker T. Washington and W. E. B. DuBois. Washington urged blacks to learn a trade instead of rocking the political boat by demanding equal rights. DuBois, on the other hand, urged blacks to pursue political and economic parity with whites. The ongoing debate culminated at a historic meeting of the two men at Carnegie Hall in January 1904.

Meanwhile, African Americans began making their mark in American theater. The African Grove on Bleecker and Mercer Streets was the earliest known all-black theater company in New York, producing Shakespearean plays from 1821 to 1829. By the late 1800s productions written and performed by blacks were showing on Broadway. The wildly successful play *Clorindy: The Origin of the Cakewalk* (1898), by Will Marion Cook and Paul Laurence Dunbar, spawned a popular dance called the cakewalk. Comedian Bert Williams and dancer George Walker produced several Broadway hits featuring black actors and dancers including *Sons of Ham* (1900), *In Dahomey* (1902), and *In Abyssinia* (1908).

Broadway was not the only place blacks were achieving recognition. A number of black inventors in New York City in the early

1900s made major contributions. Granville T. Woods invented a system of telegraphy between moving trains, and worked with Alexander Graham Bell, the inventor of the telephone, and Thomas Edison, the inventor of electricity. Woods also invented the third rail, which enabled trains to run by electricity rather than steam. Lewis Latimer was also involved with Bell and the telephone. Latimer created the drawings for the telephone Bell patented. In 1881 Latimer patented his own invention—carbon filament for the first incandescent electric light bulb.

HARLEM

Dutch farmers Isaac and Hendrick De Forest were the first to settle the area north of New Amsterdam, around East 125th Street, in 1637. The village of Nieuw Haarlem was established in 1658 when other settlers discovered that the fertile land was ideal for farming. In the 1800s wealthy businessmen and politicians built country estates in and around Harlem in an attempt to escape the overcrowding, disease, and dirt of the city. An example of a country estate of this era is Hamilton Grange, the home of Alexander Hamilton, located at 141st Street and Convent Avenue. (Hamilton, a graduate of Kings College—now Columbia College of Columbia University—was author of the Federalist Papers and the first secretary of the Treasury under President Washington.) Today visitors can explore the Hamilton Heights Historic District from West 142nd Street to West 145th Street, between Amsterdam and St. Nicholas Avenues.

The Greek Revival-influenced Morris-Jumel Mansion on 160th Street and Edgecombe Avenue is another example of a colonial country estate. This hillside mansion was built in 1765 as the summer home of British officer Roger Morris and his wife, and was later purchased in 1810 by French merchant Stephen Jumel and his wife Eliza. The house was Washington's temporary head-quarters during the Battle of Harlem Heights.

Harlem's evolution from sparsely populated farmland in the 1600s and 1700s to suburban country estates in the 1800s was just the beginning. By 1900 a large migration to Harlem was spurred by the construction of New York's elevated train—the IRT Lenox Avenue line on the West Side. In 1904 the line was extended to 148th Street. Improvements in the transportation system made it easier for white businessmen and their families to move north to Harlem, a cleaner, less congested community. A building boom began when apartment buildings and row houses were constructed at an alarming rate to accommodate the surge in population of primarily German, Irish, Jewish, and Italian families. The stream of white families to the Harlem suburb slowed after an economic downturn, which burdened the landlords and owners with a massive inventory of beautiful but vacant apartments. Enterprising black realtor Philip A. Payton approached the frustrated speculators with a proposal to rent their empty apartments to blacks. Reluctant at first, but eager when they realized that they could charge higher rents, the white owners agreed to Payton's proposal. Speculators, both black and white, participated in the ensuing real estate bonanza from 1904 to 1908. St. Philip's Epis-copal Church, one of the wealthiest black churches in Harlem, pur-chased thirteen buildings on 135th Street between Lenox and Seventh Avenues, and Payton and his business partner, J. C. Thomas, bought two apartment buildings and dispossessed the white tenants in order to rent to blacks. Blacks moved from the Tenderloin and San Juan Hill sections in midtown Manhattan, fleeing the poor living conditions described in the December 1900 issue of *Harper's Weekly:*

> Property is not rented to Negroes in New York until white people will no longer have it. Then rents are put up from thirty to fifty per cent, and Negroes are permitted to take a street or sometimes a neighborhood. There are really not many Negro sections, and all that exist are fearfully crowded. . . .

They [the landlords] charge enormous rentals for very inferior houses and tenements, which yield more when the negroes have taken possession than they did in time of seemingly greater prosperity. . . .

Moreover, they make no repairs, and the property usually goes to rack and ruin. . . . As a rule . . . Negroes in New York are not beholden to the property owners for anything except discomfort and extortion. . . .

Harlem became a haven for blacks. The beautiful row houses and elegant apartment buildings were better than any of the housing blacks had lived in previously in New York City. African American writer James Weldon Johnson described Harlem in the early 1900s in his book *Black Manhattan:*

Harlem is one of the most beautiful and healthful sites in the whole city. It is not a slum, nor is it a "quarter" consisting of dilapidated tenements. It is a section of new-law apartment houses and handsome dwellings, with streets as well paved, as well lighted, and as well kept as in any other part of the city.

The black churches like St. Philip's Episcopal Church, Mother A.M.E. Zion Church, Abyssinian Baptist Church, and others followed their flocks and moved to Harlem from their downtown locations. Black entertainers Scott Joplin, Jim Europe, Bert Williams, W. C. Handy, and Eubie Blake moved to Harlem to be close to the action. The National Association for the Advancement of Colored People (NAACP) and the Urban League, organizations aimed at the betterment of the black race, were founded in New York City in 1909 and 1910, respectively. Their publications *Crisis,* the magazine of the NAACP, and *Opportunity,* the magazine of the National Urban League, covered racial issues affecting blacks and published the works of African American poets and authors in their pages.

By 1910 Harlem was the second largest black community in the United States, after Washington, D.C. This large black community was a perfect place for Marcus Garvey to organize a branch of his Universal Negro Improvement Association (UNIA) in 1918. Garvey, an ardent believer in black separatism and racial uplift, preached that blacks should return to Africa and reclaim it in the wake of what he declared the end of European colonialism. Garvey's 5,000-seat auditorium, Liberty Hall at 120 West 138th Street, was the location of the UNIA's first convention, where delegates from the United States, the West Indies, and Africa discussed the creation of a black economy. Garvey created a weekly newspaper, the *Negro World,* the Black Star Line, a shipping company that transported blacks to Africa, and an array of businesses, including a grocery store, laundry and dressmaking shop, restaurant, bakery, and publishing house. Labeled a radical and dissident by the Justice Department, Garvey was put under surveillance and the UNIA was infiltrated by government agents. Garvey was convicted of mail fraud in 1924 and served three years of a five-year sentence before being deported to Jamaica in 1927.

When the United States entered World War I in 1917, the New York City workforce changed significantly. European immigration slowed and jobs traditionally held by new immigrants were now being filled by women and blacks who had migrated from the South and the West Indies.

The majority of black soldiers who served in the war were assigned to all-black labor and engineering battalions. The exception was an outstanding black regiment from Harlem, the New York National Guard's 15th Regiment, which became the 369th Infantry. Assigned to the French Army, the 369th Infantry, also known as the Harlem Hellfighters, fought heroically in Germany and garnered French honors for their bravery, including the croix de guerre. The regiment was also famous for its band, led by Jim Reese Europe, which introduced jazz to the French, beginning an enduring relationship between black jazz artists and French audi-

Jim Reese Europe led the 369th Infantry Band up Fifth Avenue on the return of the Harlem Hellfighters to Harlem from World War I. Pictured is Jim Europe's string sextet around 1920. (Courtesy of Stuart Reid & Family)

ences. After the war ended, the triumphant 369th Infantry marched up Fifth Avenue in February 1919 with tap dancer Bill "Bojangles" Robinson as its drum major.

The euphoria surrounding the return of troops to New York was short-lived for blacks. Racial unrest grew after World War I, and riots and lynchings occurred in American cities, including Chicago, Washington, D.C., and in the South. Harlem resident and black poet Claude McKay wrote his seminal poem, "If We Must Die," in response to the tensions.

By 1920, two-thirds of Manhattan's black population of more than 100,000 lived in Harlem. A magnet for talented black poets and writers like Langston Hughes, Countee Cullen, Zora Neale Hurston, Rudolph Fisher, and Wallace Thurman, musicians like Fats Waller, Eubie Blake, and Duke Ellington, and artists like Augusta Savage, Aaron Douglass, and Richmond Barthé, Harlem became the center of a black cultural revolution. From 1920 to 1930 the population of blacks in Harlem more than doubled, with most of the new residents coming from the South. This period of growth and immense creativity and productivity in the arts was called the Harlem Renaissance.

On Broadway, Eubie Blake and Noble Sissle's smash hit *Shuffle Along* (1921) was piquing interest in black culture. Carl Van Vechten's bestselling novel *Nigger Heaven* (1925), about Negro life in Harlem, fueled white fascination in all things black. These two works offered a view into black life and people wanted more. Curiosity spurred a stampede of whites, who were referred to as "slummers," to Harlem in search of music, booze, race mixing, and a good time. The Volstead Act of 1920 outlawed the sale of alcohol, but that was a mere technicality for club owners in Harlem. During Prohibition many of the clubs, owned and operated by white mobsters, sold bootlegged liquor to their clientele. The famed Cotton Club and Connie's Inn, which catered only to white patrons, Small's Paradise, where the waiters and waitresses served customers on roller skates, and Minton's Playhouse (the birthplace of bebop in the 1940s), were just some of the clubs frequented by slummers that epitomized the sensuosity and raucousness of black cabaret life.

The stock market crash of 1929 signaled the end of the good times for everyone in America, including the residents of Harlem. The Depression that followed the crash wreaked havoc on the overpopulated community. Families now had to live two and three to an apartment, and often hosted "rent parties"—where revelers paid an admission price to eat, drink, and be merry—in order to raise money for the high rents. Food was scarce, and discrimination made it nearly impossible for blacks to compete for the few employment opportunities that existed. Families were forced to rely on public assistance to meet their basic needs. Congestion and substandard housing took its toll, and tuberculosis became the number-one killer of blacks in the 1930s. Crime increased, and tensions brought about by prolonged poverty, unemployment, discrimination, and poor housing conditions finally culminated in a riot on March 19, 1935. Ten thousand blacks burned and looted stores owned by white merchants after a rumor in the community claimed that a young boy caught stealing at a department store on 125th Street had been beaten to death. The rumor was false, but that was of little consequence to the rioters, who were frustrated by the high unemployment rate, pervasive discrimination, and exorbitant rents for substandard housing.

Adam Clayton Powell Jr., the pastor of Abyssinian Baptist Church beginning in 1937, emerged as an outspoken social and political leader in the Harlem community with his "Don't Buy Where You Can't Work" campaigns during the 1930s. He led successful boycotts against the white merchants, the utility company, and the 1939 World's Fair for refusing to hire blacks. As a result of Powell's boycotts, blacks were eventually hired by merchants, the utility company, and the World's Fair. Powell was elected to New York's City Council in 1941, where he served two terms before moving onto the national stage as a member of the U.S. House of Representatives in 1944. As chairman of the Education and Labor Committee, he held the honor of being the first black to head up a major congressional committee. Powell was a controversial figure, who was actually thrown out of Congress for allegedly misusing campaign funds; however, he was quickly reelected and served until 1970, when he was defeated by Charles Rangel.

Rangel, another powerful black politician from Harlem, who still serves in the House as of 2001, was a former U.S. attorney and New York State assemblyman. He was named chairman of the Congressional Black Caucus in 1974. As a member of the House Judiciary Committee, he participated in the Nixon impeachment hearings, and in 1975 he became the first African American to be appointed to the prestigious and powerful House Ways and Means Committee.

There was some good news in the 1930s for blacks in New York. Joe Louis, "the Brown Bomber," became heavyweight champion of the world in 1937. The title was a mantle of pride worn by each and every black person in America.

But pride was not enough to guarantee jobs and equality with whites. In 1941, as America prepared for World War II, black protesters demanded jobs in the defense industry. It was not until 1941, threatened by a scheduled black march on Washington spearheaded by A. Philip Randolph (political activist and founder of the Brotherhood of Sleeping Car Porters and Maids) that President Franklin D. Roosevelt signed an executive order opening defense jobs to blacks. More black men and women enlisted in the armed services during World War II than in World War I, but the troops remained segregated. The U.S. Armed Forces were not desegregated until 1948, under the Truman administration.

Blacklisting and Senator Joseph McCarthy's Red Scare distinguished the 1950s. The so-called McCarthy hearings in the House Committee on Un-American Activities, which aimed to out members of the Communist Party and their sympathizers, had its effect on Harlem. Actor-singer-activist Paul Robeson and educator-scholar W. E. B. DuBois were forced to surrender their passports amid accusations of communist activities. Robeson could no longer travel, which ultimately destroyed his career. DuBois was jailed, tried, and acquitted.

In 1954 the Supreme Court reached its landmark decision to desegregate schools in Brown v. the Board of Education. Thurgood Marshall led the NAACP's legal defense team in this historic fight, and later became the first African American appointed to the Supreme Court.

Harlem deteriorated in the fifties and sixties as a result of absentee landlords, crime, and drugs. Many black families moved to the Hunts Point, Morrisania, Tremont, Melrose, and Highbridge sections of the Bronx, and many others to Jamaica, St. Albans, Hollis, Corona, and later Laurelton and Cambria Heights in Queens.

Malcolm X arrived in Harlem in 1954 to head the Harlem Branch of the Nation of Islam. Headquartered at Temple #7, Malcolm preached a message of black unity and economic development. A mesmerizing speaker, Malcolm recruited thousands of young black men into the Muslim faith. Clean-shaven, bowtie-wearing young men hawked *Muhammad Speaks,* the Muslim newspaper, and bean pies from the streets of Harlem. As Malcolm X became more powerful, his relationship with the Honorable Elijah Muhammed, the Chicago-based leader of the movement, became strained. Malcolm left the Nation of Islam in 1964 and formed the Organization of Afro-American Unity, headquartered in the Theresa Hotel. Malcolm X was assassinated on February 21, 1965, while giving a speech at the Audubon Ballroom in upper Manhattan.

The 1960s were tumultuous times for African Americans. The summer of 1964 was the beginning of many summers of black discontent. Riots plagued major cities from New York to Los Angeles. Fires and looting caused millions of dollars worth of damage in Harlem and Brooklyn. Civil rights organizations pursued equality for blacks in education, employment, and housing, as well as voting rights for blacks in the South. The NAACP, Martin Luther King's Southern Christian Leadership Conference (SCLC), and Stokely Carmichael's Student Nonviolent Coordinating Committee (SNCC) were magnets for New York's black activists, who joined the struggle for equality and raised money and awareness, and changed laws.

Martin Luther King was a frequent visitor to New York City during the sixties. He picketed with the hospital workers union 1199 in 1964, spoke against the Vietnam War at the Riverside Church in 1967, and made an address at Carnegie Hall in 1968, a month before he was assassinated, to commemorate the birthday of scholar W. E. B. DuBois.

The assassinations of Malcolm X (February 21, 1965) and Martin Luther King (April 4, 1968) lent a militancy and urgency to black demands for social change. The next two decades brought an increase in black elected officials in New York City. Brooklynite Shirley Chisholm was elected to the U.S. House of Representatives in 1968, and, in 1972, she made a bid for the presidency of the United States, becoming the first woman and the first black to seek that office. Harlem's Percy Sutton became Manhattan Borough President in 1968. Mr. Sutton would later become the owner of Inner City Broadcasting Company, the parent company of radio stations WLIB-AM and WBLS-FM. But it was not until over twenty years later that New York elected its first black mayor. David N. Dinkins, former Manhattan Borough President, took office in 1989, but lost his bid for reelection in 1993 to Republican challenger Rudolph Giuliani.

The Giuliani administration has been trying for the black citizens of New York. There has been a dramatic increase in police brutality incidents in which blacks were victimized and abused by white police officers. As these incidents involving blacks and the police made headlines in the local and national press, Reverend Al Sharpton, a contemporary political activist, has emerged as a prominent community leader. Sharpton has led thousands of marchers in protest against the injustices suffered by black New Yorkers.

There have been many highly-charged cases that Sharpton has brought before the national conscience: the Howard Beach incident (December 20, 1986), in which Michael Griffith was killed by a car as he and his friends were chased by a white mob toting weapons; the Abner Louima attack (August 9, 1997), in which a Haitian immigrant was sodomized by a white policeman while in custody; and the Amadou Diallo murder (February 4, 1999), in which a young, unarmed African man was shot down by New York City policemen.

As of the 2000 census, the population of Manhattan is 1,537,195; of that total, there are 267,302 black or African American residents. Although black New Yorkers face challenges daily on many fronts, their contributions to the community at large continue to be important threads in the fabric of this large and diverse city.

MANHATTAN

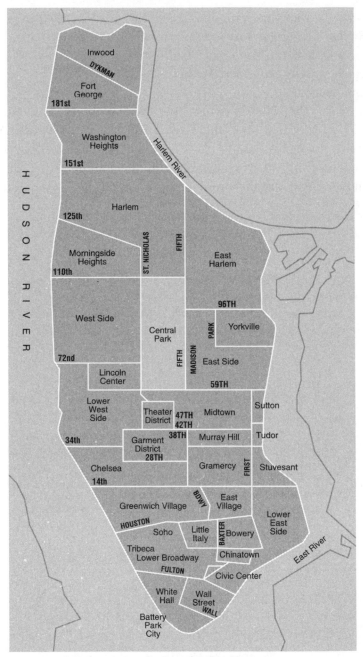

1

Manhattan

MANHATTAN ITINERARY

A great way to get into New York's early history is to start in Lower Manhattan, at the actual tip of the island. Visitors can take the subway to the Bowling Green stop, which leaves you off right at New York's oldest park. The tiny park, laid out as an actual bowling green in 1733, is located directly in front of the U.S. Customs House, now the home of the Smithsonian's National Museum of the American Indian. To the left of the Customs House is historic Battery Park—where gun batteries were once kept—now a beautifully designed waterfront green built on landfill, where you can see the Walloon Memorial and the Immigrants sculpture in front of Castle Clinton. Through the entrance of Castle Clinton, a fort built 100 yards offshore before the land was filled in, visitors can purchase tickets and board the ferry to Liberty Park, home of the Statue of Liberty.

Exit Battery Park at Pearl Street, which is on the east side of the park, and walk a short distance to the site of Fraunces Tavern at 54 Pearl Street, where George Washington gave his farewell speech on December 4, 1783, to his soldiers. The owner of the tavern at the time was Samuel Fraunces, known as "Black Sam." An immi-

Bowling Green, lower Manhattan
(Photo by Linda Tarrant-Reid)

grant from the West Indies, Sam is believed to have been black. A museum and gift shop are located on the second floor, and the first floor was formerly a restaurant, which is scheduled to reopen, with decor in the style of an English dining room. (See page 35.)

From the tavern, walk north on Broad Street to Wall Street, then west to the intersection of Wall and Broadway to see Trinity Church, established in 1697. St. Philips Episcopal Church in Harlem has its roots in this historic church. (See page 77.)

Another important site, the John Street Methodist Church at 44 John Street, is within walking distance. Walk north on Broadway and make a right at John Street. Walk a block and a half and find the colonial church founded in 1766, in the middle of the block between Nassau and William Streets. This was the first Methodist congregation in North America and the church where

The Immigrants statue, in Battery Park (Photo by Linda Tarrant-Reid)

ex-slave Peter Williams was sexton. Williams was one of the founders of the African Methodist Episcopal Zion Church, Mother A.M.E. Zion, which is now located in Harlem. The small museum in the basement of the church has paintings, furnishings, and memorabilia documenting the church's early history. The balcony where black worshippers sat during service, segregated from the rest of the congregation, is still intact. (See page 73.)

During the week, Nassau Street is closed to vehicular traffic and you can enjoy, on foot, many of its shops, restaurants, and street vendors that cater to the lunch-hour throngs in the financial district.

The historic South Street Seaport on the East River is another must-see destination for visitors, with its beautiful harbor view and lovely shops and eateries. Just head east down John Street after visiting the church—it's only four blocks to where the seaport shops begin.

You might want to take a cab over to the City Hall area next. City Hall at 51 Chambers Street and the surrounding area is the site of the first African community in New York after slavery was abolished in the state in 1827. Named the Five Points District, the neighborhood was home to many black-owned businesses and social organizations. Today, with the proliferation of giant office complexes and renumbering of the streets, there is very little left that attests to this history. However, if you travel north up to Reade Street, turn right and then go left on Elk Street, you'll see the small park memorializing the African Burial Ground, where blacks were buried from about 1712 to 1794. (See below.)

Next you might want to head north to Soho, an exciting neighborhood, and check out the James Brown House, built by black tobacconist James Brown in 1817, at 326 Spring Street near the West Side Highway. The building, which now houses pub-restaurant the Ear Inn, is a New York City landmark and a designated historic place. Brown was an aide to General Washington during the Revolutionary War, and is believed to be pictured in the famous painting *The Crossing of the Delaware* by Emanuel Leuze which hangs in the Metropolitan Museum of Art. The Ear Inn does not pay homage to its original occupant in decor or dishes, but the owner does know a little bit about the history of the place. It's a great spot to catch a bite to eat, and, if you're lucky, maybe a story or two about the past inhabitants of the James Brown House.

HISTORIC SITES AND LANDMARKS

AFRICAN BURIAL GROUND
Elk Street (east of Broadway,
    between Duane and Reade Streets)
(212) 432-5707

In 1991 the General Services Administration broke ground for a 34-story, $276 million office complex, unearthing the remains of

The African Burial Ground, on Elk Street, east of Broadway (Photo by Linda Tarrant-Reid)

20,000 enslaved and free blacks who had been buried in colonial times in a 6-acre plot of land referred to as the Negroes Burying Ground. The burial ground was in use from about 1712 to 1794, after Trinity Church declared that blacks would no longer be buried in its churchyard.

With the discovery of the historic site, construction was halted and a cultural survey conducted. Approximately 408 intact remains of men, women, and children were recovered from the neighborhood, formerly known as Republican Alley. The remains were removed and stored at first at Lehman College in the Bronx, but were later moved to Howard University in Washington, D.C. Although public outcry did not stop construction of the office building, it did succeed in halting the planned construction of an adjacent 4-story pavilion, and the burial ground was later designated a national historic landmark. On the site proposed for the pavilion is a memorial marker that describes the burial ground. Plans for the construction of a more formal memorial are in the works. Groups of ten or more can tour the site.

TRINITY CHURCH

74 Trinity Place (Broadway at Wall Street)
(212) 602-0800
www.trinitychurchwallstreet.org

Established in 1697 as an Anglican church, the graveyard of Trinity Church is believed to be the first cemetery where Africans were buried until they were given their own burial ground north of City Hall, today known as the African Burial Ground. St. Philip's Episcopal, in Harlem, was established in 1818 by black parishioners of Trinity who were tired of being separated from white parishioners during worship service.

JOHN STREET METHODIST CHURCH

44 John Street (between Nassau and Williams Streets)

Peter Williams (1748–1823), a slave owned by the Trustees of Wesley Chapel (John Street Church), purchased his freedom from the church and served as its sexton from 1776 to 1787. (Courtesy of John Street Church)

Founded in 1766, this is the oldest Methodist church in the United States. Ex-slave Peter Williams was the church's first sexton. Williams, who was bought by the church after his master returned to Britain, purchased his own freedom from the church and became a tobacconist, undertaker, and one of the founders of Mother A.M.E. Zion Church, now located in Harlem. There is a small museum in the basement of the church that displays a picture of Peter Williams, as well as artifacts, memorabilia, and documents of the church's colonial history.

James Brown House at 326 Spring Street in lower
Manhattan (Photo by Linda Tarrant-Reid)

JAMES BROWN HOUSE
326 Spring Street (between Greenwich
  and Washington Streets)
(212) 219-8026

This classic Federal-style house with a brick façade and gambrel
roof was built in 1817 and was the home of James Brown, a free
black man who was an aide to George Washington during the Revolutionary War. It is one of the few sites left that represents the his-

tory of African Americans in colonial days in New York City. After the war, Brown built the house, a wooden post and beam construction, and opened a tobacco store on the first floor. The upstairs apartment, which is not open to the public, is in its original condition, with spruce floor planks, doors, and fireplace mantle. Designated a New York City landmark in 1964 and placed on the National Register of Historic Places in 1979, the James Brown House is currently facing one of its biggest challenges. Currently a pub called the Ear Inn, where the likes of Salvador Dali, John Lennon, and Tom Waits were known to hoist a few, the structure is in danger of collapsing due to the Department of Transportation's work on a water main right outside its door. (See page 31.)

The following sites are historic, but have no formal marker to indicate their historic significance. In some cases, the original buildings no longer exist due to development in the area.

FREEDOM'S JOURNAL
152 Church Street (at Leonard Street)

This address was the location of *Freedom's Journal*, the first black-owned newspaper published in the United States. Founded by John Russwurm and Rev. Samuel Cornish in 1827, the newspaper was located at Zion Church which was later named Mother A.M.E. Zion Church. It stopped publication only two years later in 1829, but spawned many other black publications.

DAVID RUGGLES HOME
36 Lispenard Street

This was the home of abolitionist David Ruggles (1820–1849), an active participant on the Underground Railroad who helped scores of fugitive slaves escape to Canada. Ruggles also owned a bookstore at number 67 Lispenard, where blacks came to read because they were not permitted to use the public libraries. A white mob set the store on fire in 1835, a year after it opened. In 1838 Ruggles began a black quarterly, *Mirror of Liberty*. He also founded the New York Vigilance Committee, which protected free blacks from being kidnapped by slave catchers. In 1839 Ruggles published the *Slaveholders Directory*, a listing of the names and addresses of politicians, lawyers, and police in New York who "[lent] themselves to kidnapping."

NEW YORK AFRICAN SOCIETY FOR MUTUAL RELIEF
42 Baxter Street

This organization was founded in 1784 to offer its members intellectual stimulation and an environment of support. It was the first organization to be incorporated by black Americans. The society provided insurance and financial aid to its members, their families, and to others who needed assistance. The membership was made up of artisans, bootmakers, mechanics, real estate salesmen, and other professionals. The Baxter Street headquarters, which was built in 1818, also served as a station on the Underground Railroad. The organization later moved to 27 Greenwich Street.

AFRICAN FREE SCHOOLS
245 William Street (near Duane Street)
137 Mulberry Street (near Grand Street)

The African Free Schools were founded by the New York Manumission Society in 1787 to educate black children. The first school, located on William Street between Beekman and Ferry Streets, was destroyed by fire in 1814, and a second school at 245 William Street was built in 1815. John Jay and Alexander Hamilton were among the society's founding members. The Mulberry Street School for Girls and Boys was established in 1820. By 1834, the African Free Schools became part of the New York City Public School Society, which began to finance them.

FIVE POINTS DISTRICT
Near City Hall and surrounding streets

The Five Points District, the area around Worth, Centre, and Bayard Streets, near City Hall, was the first community where freed blacks lived after slavery was abolished in New York in 1827. This area was a slum of shanty houses, where disease, poverty, and crime were rampant among the black and Irish residents. The first black churches were established in this area. Abyssinian Baptist Church, founded in 1808, was located on what is now Worth Street, Mother A.M.E. Zion, founded in 1796, was at Leonard and Church Streets, and St. Philip's Episcopal Church, established in 1818, was on Centre Street.

AFRICAN GROVE
Corner of Mercer and Bleecker Streets

The African Grove presented plays produced and acted by black actors for African American audiences from 1821 to 1830. Playwright Henry Brown was the artistic director of this unique company that performed Shakespearean plays including *Othello, Richard III,* and *Hamlet.* James Hewlett was the company's principal singer, and it is believed that the internationally renowned black actor Ira Aldridge also performed at the Grove.

SENECA VILLAGE SITE
The Great Lawn at Central Park (park entrance at 85th Street and Central Park West)

Shards of pottery and glass, Chinese porcelain, and oyster shells were uncovered when the Great Lawn of Central Park was renovated in 1997. These bits of history are all that is left of a community of African Americans who lived on this land from about 1825 until 1857, when construction began on Central Park.

According to property records, on September 27, 1825, Andrew Williams purchased three lots from John and Elizabeth Whitehead for the sum of $125 per lot. During that same time, trustees from the Mother A.M.E. Zion Church purchased six lots near 86th Street to use as a cemetery for black people. And Epiphany Davis, another trustee of the Mother A.M.E. Zion Church, purchased twelve lots for $578. It is believed that the African Americans purchased the land so that they could vote. In New York City at that time, one had to be not only a resident but also a landowner and a taxpayer to cast a vote. In the 1840s, Seneca Village's population grew with the migration of the Irish to New York. By all accounts, this was a harmonious community with three churches, one public school, and three cemeteries.

MUSEUMS AND GALLERIES

FRAUNCES TAVERN AND MUSEUM
54 Pearl Street (at Broad Street)

The Tavern, built in 1719, was the site of General Washington's farewell address to his troops on December 4, 1783, at the end of the Revolutionary War. Samuel Francis, "Black Sam," owned what was then called the Queen's Head Tavern. Sam was from the French West Indies and is believed to have been a black man.

Legend has it that Sam's daughter Phoebe saved General Washington from eating poisoned peas. Washington's bodyguard, Thomas Hickey, had poisoned the vegetables and, after he was exposed by Phoebe, was hanged for his deed. Sam was appointed the first steward to the president at the New York White House at 3 Cherry Street in Manhattan.

The Fraunces Tavern museum consists of two rooms with eighteenth- and nineteenth-century furnishings and articles of American history. The museum is currently closed while the tavern is being renovated, but visitors can still view the outside of this historic structure. (See page 47.)

MUSEUM FOR AFRICAN ART
593 Broadway (between Houston and Prince Streets)
(212) 966-1313

The museum offers changing exhibitions of historical and contemporary African art, including sculptures, masks, artifacts, and costumes. Also, special programs for schools, families, and individuals featuring films and video, music, dance, and performance art are available every Friday evening. Hands-on workshops are offered on Saturdays.

Open Wednesday through Sunday, 11:00 A.M. to 6:00 P.M.; Friday and Saturday, 11:00 A.M. to 8:00 P.M. Admission: $4; $2 students, seniors, and kids. Call for more information.

MUSEUM OF MODERN ART (MOMA)
11 West 53rd Street (between Fifth and Sixth Avenues)
(212) 708-9480
www.moma.org

MOMA's collection includes over 100,000 paintings, sculptures, drawings, prints, illustrated books, architectural models, design objects, photographs, and films. The permanent collection has thirty works by African American artist Jacob Lawrence, which are part of a series of panels entitled *Migration of the Negro*. Call for information on current exhibitions. The museum also offers live jazz performances on Friday evenings—for information, call (212) 798-9491.

Open Monday, Tuesday, Thursday, Saturday, and Sunday from 10:30 A.M. to 5:45 P.M.; Fridays, 10:30 A.M. to 8:15 P.M. Admission: $10, $6.50 students with ID and seniors 65+; free for kids under sixteen, accompanied by an adult.

Metropolitan Museum of Art
1000 Fifth Avenue (at 82nd Street)
(212) 535-7710
www.metmusem.org

The museum's collection spans 5,000 years of art and culture, including the golden civilizations of ancient Egypt, Africa, Europe, and the Americas. The museum has artistic works by African American artists Horace Pippin, Jacob Lawrence, and Richmond Barthé. Also in the Met's permanent collection is the African Gallery (in the Rockefeller Wing), where the art of western and central Africa is housed. The bronze, ivory, and wood sculptures from the Benin, Dogon, and Bamama peoples are magnificent. A collection of African musical instruments displayed in the Mertens Gallery consists of lutes, drums, gourds, rattles, and thumb pianos.

Open Tuesday through Thursday and Sunday from 9:30 A.M. to 5:30 P.M.; Friday and Saturday, 9:30 A.M. to 9:00 P.M. Suggested admission: $10; $5 students and seniors; free for members and kids under twelve.

Museum of the City of New York
1220 Fifth Avenue (at 103rd Street)
(212) 534-1672
www.mcny.org

Located on New York City's Museum Mile, this eclectic museum features three centuries of paintings, prints, photographs, silver, furniture, costumes, dollhouses, fire trucks, and theatrical memorabilia that tell the story of New York City from Dutch Colonial days to the present. The museum's changing exhibitions have focused on prominent African Americans such as photographer Gordon Parks and actor-singer-activist Paul Robeson. The permanent collection of Broadway memorabilia details the contributions of African Americans to New York theater.

Open Wednesday through Sunday; Tuesdays for tours and organized groups. The gift shop is open during museum hours. Admission: $5; $4 students, seniors, and kids; $10 families.

MUSEUM OF TELEVISION AND RADIO
25 West 52nd Street (between Fifth and Sixth Avenues)
(212) 621-6600
www.mtr.org

With a collection of more than 60,000 television and radio programs,
including news, performing arts, children's programs, sports, and
public affairs, visitors are transported back in time to the beginning
of the electronic media age. The museum has art galleries, screening rooms, and theaters for their special programs. Visitors can
screen some of the first television programs hosted by or starring
African Americans, such as singer Nat King Cole's early musical variety show and Diahann Carroll's half-hour program *Julia,* about a
widowed mother raising her son. There are also special exhibitions,
seminars, and screenings and workshops on the weekends for kids.

Open Tuesday through Sunday, Noon to 6:00 P.M. Suggested
admission: $6; $4 students and seniors; $3 kids under thirteen; free
for members.

WHITNEY MUSEUM OF AMERICAN ART
945 Madison Avenue (at 75th Street)
(212) 570-3676
www.whitney.org

The museum's collection includes the works of African American
artists Charles White, Richmond Barthé, and Jacob Lawrence. The
museum store, bookstore, and restaurant are also open during
museum hours.

Open Tuesday, Wednesday, Thursday, Saturday and Sunday from
11:00 A.M. to 6:00 P.M.; Friday, 1:00 P.M. to 9:00 P.M. Fab Fridays

are from 6:00 P.M. to 9:00 P.M., where you can enjoy food, drink, and fun. Admission: $10; $8 students with ID and seniors; free for members and kids under twelve. Thursday is pay what you wish.

June Kelly Gallery
591 Broadway (between Houston and Prince Streets)
(212) 226-1660

This black-owned gallery exhibits contemporary paintings, sculpture, and photography by a diverse group of artists, and mounts eleven shows a year. Every May, a guest speaker presents a talk called "The Fine Art of Collection."

Open Tuesday through Saturday. Free admission. Call for more information.

Merton D. Simpson Gallery
38 West 28th Street (between Sixth Avenue and Broadway)
(212) 988-6290

This East Side gallery presents revolving exhibits twice a year in November and May. Its collection features early African and tribal art from the seventeenth, eighteenth, and nineteenth centuries. The gallery also showcases modern African American masters including Romare Bearden, Norman Lewis, and Henry Tanner.

Open Tuesday through Saturday. Free admission.

Cinque Gallery
560 Broadway (at Prince Street), 5th Floor
(212) 966-3464

Three African American artists—Romare Bearden, Ernest Crichlow, and Norman Lewis—founded the gallery in 1969 to create an environment for the promotion of minority artists. Exhibits showcase the work of emerging and mid-career artists, including painters, sculptors, ceramicists, printmakers, and photographers.

Cinque also sponsors educational outreach programs, internships, lectures, and seminars.

Open Tuesday through Saturday. Free admission.

CULTURAL CENTERS

NEW FEDERAL THEATRE (ABRONS CENTER)
466 Grand Street (between Pitt and Willetts Streets)
(212) 353-1176
www.metrobase.com/newfederal

Located on the Lower East Side, this community-based professional theater was founded in 1970 by Woodie King Jr. to provide emerging playwrights, minority actors, directors, and designers with a venue at which to present their work. Playwrights Ron Milner, Ed Bullins, J.e. Franklin, and Ntozake Shange are just a few of the talented writers whose works have been performed at NFT. Some of the actors who have performed in New Federal Theatre productions include Denzel Washington, Laurence Fishburne, Debbie Allen, Phylicia Rashad, Morgan Freeman, and Robert Downey Jr. NFT offers workshops in playwriting and drama for adults and teens. Call for more information.

NUYORICAN POETS CAFE
236 East 3rd Street (between Avenues B and C)
(212) 505-8183
www.nuyorican.org

"A living room hosting the freshest art to come through the ports of NYC, from not only the Caribbean and the Americas, but from all over the world," boasts the cafe's Web site. A meeting place for the exchange of cross-cultural art, this performance space was founded in 1975 by Miguel Algarin to provide a stage for poets,

Alvin Ailey American Dance Theater (Photo by Andrew Eccles)

writers, actors, performance artists, musicians, and visual artists. Call for more information or visit their Web site.

ALVIN AILEY AMERICAN DANCE THEATER
211 West 61st Street
(212) 767-0590

This internationally-acclaimed modern dance company, founded in 1958 by Alvin Ailey with the aim of bringing black dancers into the mainstream, is now under the direction of former principal dancer Judith Jamison. Renowned for such dance presentations as *Revelations* and *Cry*, the troupe performs works of contemporary choreographers, including both Jamison and Ailey. Call for a performance schedule and locations.

CARNEGIE HALL
881 7th Avenue (at 57th Street)
(212) 247-7800
www.carnegiehall.org

This historic concert hall has hosted concerts by African American entertainers from Duke Ellington to rhythm-and-blues diva Patti LaBelle. It is also the hall where black contralto Marian Anderson performed her last concert in 1965. That same year, South African musicians Miriam Makeba and Hugh Masekela also performed here.

Tours are available Monday, Tuesday, Thursday, and Friday. Call for a performance schedule, or visit their Web site.

The Rose Museum (154 West 57th Street, 2nd floor), is a small museum devoted to the history of Carnegie Hall. Opened in 1991 to celebrate the 100th anniversary of the hall, it houses over 300 artifacts, including memorabilia from appearances by Martin Luther King Jr., Billie Holiday, Duke Ellington, and Ella Fitzgerald.

The museum is open Monday, Tuesday, Thursday, Friday, Saturday and Sunday from 11:00 A.M. to 4:30 P.M.

LINCOLN CENTER FOR THE PERFORMING ARTS
Lincoln Center Plaza (between 62nd and 65th Streets)
(212) 875-5000

This performing arts complex houses Alice Tully Hall (212-875-5050); Avery Fisher Hall (212-875-5030); Juilliard School of Music (212-799-5000); Vivian Beaumont and Mitzi E. Newhouse Theaters (212-239-6200); Walter Reade Theater (212-875-5600); as well as the Metropolitan Opera House and the New York State Theater. It is the site of many cultural events, including concerts by singers, musicians, and entertainers of color. Call for a performance schedule.

Jazz at Lincoln Center presents *Jazz for Young People* (Photo by Petra)

JAZZ AT LINCOLN CENTER
Lincoln Center
33 West 60th Street
www.jazzatlincolncenter.org
(212) 258-9800

Under the artistic direction of jazz musician Wynton Marsalis, and the executive direction of Rob Gibson, Jazz at Lincoln Center produces concerts, lectures, film programs, publications, recordings, television broadcasts, radio broadcasts, and national and international tours. The program also sponsors an annual high school jazz band competition and festival, master classes, workshops, and other educational activities for people of all ages. Performances are at Lincoln Center, 140 W. 65th Street at Columbus Avenue. Call for more information.

BLACK BROADWAY

The 1921 production of the musical *Shuffle Along*, the first post-war play with music, lyrics, choreography, actors, and production by blacks, was not the first appearance by blacks on the Great White Way. Blacks had performed on Broadway in minstrel shows, such as *Creole Show* (1891) by white burlesque theater owner Sam T. Jack, and *Octoroons* and *Oriental America* by John W. Isham. These shows were revues—a series of skits and scenes of black and white comics in blackface performing demeaning routines and musical interludes—created by the black composers of the day. In 1898 Will Marion Cook and Paul Laurence Dunbar collaborated on *Clorindy—The Origin of the Cakewalk*, one of the earliest black musicals to reach Broadway. *A Trip to Coontown* by Bob Cole and William "Billy" Johnson also debuted at that time and was the first theatrical production written, produced, and acted in by all blacks. The revue consisted of songs, vaudeville acts, some opera, and John Philip Sousa's "Stars and Stripes Forever." Cole wrote the song "Boola Boola" for the show, and the ditty later became Yale University's fight song. Some of the other black productions on Broadway from 1899 to 1908 were *Jes Lak White Folks*, *In Dahomey*, *In Abyssinia*, *Sons of Ham*, and *In Bandanaland*. Will Marion Cook, a famous black composer of the period, wrote many of the scores for these plays.

The Theatre Owners Booking Association (TOBA) was founded in 1920 to facilitate the booking of black productions into black theaters, especially in the South. In the 1920s and 1930s, Harlem's Lafayette, Lincoln, and Alhambra Theaters were venues in which many black productions were mounted.

In 1921, black comedians Aubrey Lyles and Flournoy Miller wrote the book for the successful musical *Shuffle Along*, with lyrics and music by Noble Sissle and Eubie Blake. It was a Broadway smash, with a cast that included Florence Mills, Josephine Baker, Ether Walters, Paul Robeson, Hall Johnson, William Grant Still, and others.

Porgy, one of the most recognized and enduring black plays, opened on Broadway in 1927, and was followed by the wildly successful musical *Blackbirds of 1928*, with dancer Bill "Bojangles" Robinson. The European production of *Blackbirds* starred singer-dancer Florence Mills, who returned home gravely ill with acute appendicitis. Mills died shortly after her return at the age of thirty-two.

Contemporary Broadway has been the scene of some incredible plays featuring black cast members: Lorraine Hansberry's *A Raisin in the Sun*; *Purlie*; *Jelly's Last Jam*; Melvin Van Peebles's *Ain't Supposed to Die a Natural Death*; *The Wiz*; *Sophisticated Ladies*; *Dreamgirls*; *Tap Dance Kid*; *Ain't Misbehavin'*; Ntozake Shange's *For Colored Girls Who Have Considered Suicide When the Rainbow Is Enuf*; *Eubie*; August Wilson's *Ma Rainey's Black Bottom Blues* and *The Piano Lesson*; *Seven Guitars*; The Delaney Sisters' *Having Our Say*; Savion Glover's *Bring in Da Noise, Bring in Da Funk*; Joe Turner's *Come and Gone*; *Two Trains Running*; *Home*; *The Colored Museum*; *Smokey Joe's Café*; *It Ain't Nothin' But the Blues*; *The Civil War*; and many others.

Off-Broadway theaters such as the Roger Furman Theatre, the New Federal Theatre, the Billie Holiday Theatre, and La Mama have mounted productions that have, in many cases, found their way to Broadway.

For information about Broadway and off-Broadway productions, check the theater listings in the Arts and Entertainment section of the Sunday *New York Times* and the entertainment section of weekly publications such as the *Amsterdam News*, *New York* magazine, and *Time Out New York*.

MADISON SQUARE GARDEN

4 Pennsylvania Plaza (Seventh Avenue between
    31st and 33rd Streets)
(212) 465-6741
www.thegarden.com

The home of the National Basketball Association team the New York Knickerbockers, this world-famous arena is also the site of many family events, including circuses, ice skating shows, concerts, and sporting events. Tours are available. Call box office for more information.

THE THEATER AT MADISON SQUARE GARDEN

4 Pennsylvania Plaza (Seventh Avenue between
    31st and 33rd Streets)
(212) 465-6741

Within the Madison Garden Complex is this much smaller venue, which hosts plays, concerts, award programs, and other special events. The *Essence Awards,* which honors achievements of blacks from across the United States, has been broadcast from this theater since 1997. Call for more information.

RADIO CITY MUSIC HALL

Rockefeller Center
Sixth Avenue (at 50th Street)
(212) 247-4777
www.radiocity.com

This landmark theater, home to the world-famous Rockettes, is also known for its live holiday-pageant extravaganzas, including the Christmas and Easter productions, with music, singing, dancing, and elaborate costumes and sets. The theater's recent renovation has made this an even more beautiful venue for families to enjoy. Rhythm-and-blues artists Erykah Badu, Mary J. Blige, and Toni Braxton have headlined shows at this historic theater. Radio City

Music Hall has been the scene of televised award shows, rock concerts, and other special musical events. Call for tour and group sale information.

TOWN HALL
123 West 43rd Street (between Sixth Avenue and Broadway)
(212) 840-2824

This has been the venue for a variety of cultural arts programs including concerts, films, and lectures. Jazz pianist Hazel Scott and singer Paul Robeson have performed here. Call for more information.

DINING OUT

FRAUNCES TAVERN
54 Pearl Street (at Broad Street)
(212) 344-9191

This colonial tavern, located in the Wall Street area, is being renovated and will reopen around July 4, 2001. The new owners have agreed to maintain the historic ambiance of the tavern by keeping the name and by serving primarily American cuisine. They plan to expand the menu to include some West Indian dishes as a tribute to the tavern's original owner, Samuel Francis, a black man from the West Indies. Fraunces Tavern is known as the place where General George Washington bade farewell to his officers after the Revolutionary War in 1783. Call for more information. (See page 35.)

PEPPERS BAR AND GRILL
95 Leonard Street (at Broadway)
(212) 343-2824
www.citysearch.com/nyc/peppers

Located in trendy Tribeca, this attractive restaurant serves Caribbean and American cuisine. Favorite dishes include Cajun

Chicken Fettucine and Caribbean Coconut Chicken, a sliced breast of chicken in a tasty lemon, coconut curry sauce. The establishment hosts live music three times a week in the main lounge.

Open Monday through Saturday. Major credit cards accepted.

MEKKA
14 Avenue A (between Houston and 2nd Streets)
(212) 475-8500

A sister restaurant to the hip, uptown haunt The Shark Bar, this downtown location serves virtually the same menu. Entrees include Georgia Bank Farm-Raised Catfish, Shrimp Étoufée, Mekka's Honey-Dipped Fried Chicken, and Aunt Dorie's Turkey Meatloaf. Dishes are served with the traditional Southern sides of Macaroni and Cheese, Black-Eyed Peas with Smoked Turkey, Collard Greens, and String Beans.

Open seven days a week. Major credit cards accepted.

EAR INN
326 Spring Street (between Greenwich
   and Washington Streets)
(212) 226-9060; (212) 431-9750

This neighborhood pub is located in the historic James Brown House (see page 31). Although the inn does not have memorabilia or historical artifacts from the time James Brown was in residence, it's still a great place to have a bite and imagine what it was like back in the day. The menu consists of starters of Smoked Trout with Horseradish and Pickled Onions, Hummus with Pita Bread, and Country-Style Pate. Entrees are the usual pasta, fish, and chicken dishes. Due to construction in front of the building, there is a chance that it may be damaged and not be with us long. So a jaunt to the James Brown House, one of lower Manhattan's few remaining buildings representing African American history, will be well worth your while.

Open seven days a week for lunch and dinner. Major credit cards accepted.

PINK TEA CUP
42 Grove Street (between Bleecker and Bedford Streets)
(212) 807-6755

This institution has been serving the Greenwich Village community since 1954. Savor a down-home meal of grits, fried chicken, sausage, eggs, and biscuits, or go straight to the traditional soul food dishes like Fried Pork Chops with Corn Fritters, Black-Eyed Peas, Collard Greens, and Homemade Apple Pie. It's all good, especially after a night of partying.

Open seven days a week for breakfast, lunch, and dinner.

BAMBOU
243 East 14th Street (between 2nd and 3rd Avenues)
(212) 358-0012

The menu at this fine restaurant is a fusion of Caribbean and French cuisine. The starters of Pumpkin Ravioli with Callaloo Coulis, Mixed Baby Greens and Cassava Chips with a Tamarind Vinaigrette, and Crab Cake served over Avocado Butter, Chive Oil, and Balsamic Molasses Syrup are exquisite examples of the mingling of cultures. Entrees of Grilled Jerk Breast of Chicken with Avocado, Rice, and Peas, and Grilled Vegetable Roti with Curry-Sauce Dahl are dishes that epitomize the best of both worlds.

Open seven days a week. Major credit cards accepted.

JUSTIN'S
31 West 21st Street (between Fifth and Sixth Avenues)
(212) 352-0599

Named after the son of famed rap impresario Sean ("Puff Daddy," now "P. Diddy") Combs, this elegant eatery offers starters like Chicken Livers and Grits with Fried Onions, Barbecue-Glazed

Chicken Wings with Blue-Cheese Dip, as well as Lobster Bisque, Fried Oysters, and Puffy Fried Shrimp. Entrees include everything from Louisiana Seafood Gumbo, to Curried Chicken, to Smothered Pork Chops, and the standard Southern Fried Chicken.

Open for dinner seven days a week; lunch, Monday through Friday. Brunch served Sunday. Reservations recommended. Major credit cards accepted.

Lola
30 West 22nd Street (between Fifth and Sixth Avenues)
(212) 675-6700

Located in the Flatiron district, Lola describes its cuisine as eclectic American with Mediterranean, Pacific Rim, Asian, and Caribbean influences. Its gospel brunch on Saturdays and Sundays is not to be missed. Enjoy the toe-tapping, foot-stomping gospel sounds of Soul Resurrection while experiencing an array of delicious dishes. The prix fixe brunch offers a choice of ten entrees and five desserts, including Banana Tatin with Raspberry Sauce, and Chocolate Truffle Cake. A sampling of the brunch choices include Smoked Trout, Goat Cheese and Scrambled Eggs with Onion Focaccia and Spiced Fries, Lola's Fried Chicken served with Cuban Black Beans, Yellow Rice, and Plantains, and Maple-Cinnamon Challah French Toast with Crème Fraiche, Warm Maple Syrup, and Grapefruit.

Open seven days a week. Reservations recommended. Major credit cards accepted. (See page 57.)

Michael Jordan's—The Steakhouse NYC
23 Vanderbilt Avenue at 42nd Street
(Grand Central Terminal)
(212) 655-2300

Former Chicago Bulls' basketball great Michael Jordan opened this steakhouse in 1998. It serves he-man portions of steaks and chops with traditional accompaniments: Garlic Mashed Potatoes, Creamed Spinach, Crisp Fried Onions, Michael's Macaroni and Cheese, French Fries, Crimini Mushrooms with White Truffle Oil, and Baked Potato. For fish lovers, entrée choices include Steamed or Broiled Maine Lobster and Broiled Atlantic Salmon. Located on the mezzanine of the recently restored Grand Central Terminal in the heart of midtown, this is a fun, but pricey, experience.

Open seven days a week for lunch and dinner. Major credit cards accepted.

Chez Josephine
414 West 42nd Street (between Ninth
  and Tenth Avenues)
(212) 594-1925

Jean-Claude Baker, the adopted son of international singer-dancer Josephine Baker, pays homage to his late mother in this European-style bistro on Theater Row, blocks away from Port Authority Bus Terminal. The varied menu offers French cuisine with a Southern flair, such as succulent Maryland Crab Cakes, Escargot Florentine, Fried Chicken with Sweet Potato Fries, and Norwegian Herbed Salmon. Guests are transported to an intimate French boîte, just a short walk from the theater district.

Open Monday through Saturday. Reservations recommended. Major credit cards accepted.

Soul Cafe
440 West 42nd Street (between Ninth and Tenth Avenues)
(212) 244-7685

Located a few doors down from Chez Josephine on Theater Row, this trendy restaurant, co-owned by actor Malik Yoba of the former hit television series *New York Undercover,* offers appetizers like King Crab Cigars (crab legs wrapped in filo served with a tropical orange sauce) and Grilled Jerk Chicken Wings with Dipping Sauce. Entrees include Creole Catfish, either grilled or blackened, and Sweet Potato- and Plantain-Crusted Red Snapper. Side dishes include Mixed Seasonal Vegetables, Macaroni and Cheese, Seasoned Fries, Sauteed Spinach, Black-Eyed Peas and Rice, and Garlic Mashed Potatoes.

Open seven days for dinner; lunch, Thursday through Saturday. Brunch served Sunday. Major credit cards accepted.

JEZEBEL
630 Ninth Avenue (at 45th Street)
(212) 582-1045

This beautifully appointed dining room, also near the Port Authority Bus Terminal, has voluminous drapes, antique chandeliers, and lace-covered tables that transport the diner to another time and place. Decidedly Southern, and just a little bit bawdy, this restaurant offers a menu every bit as intriguing as its decor. Appetizers of Charleston She-Crab Soup, with chunks of Chesapeake crabmeat in a creamy sherry base, Crispy Chicken Livers in a Brown Southern Sauce, and Jezebel's Own Hearty Green Pea Soup are just the beginning. Main courses include a mix of seafood, fowl, and meats. Some standouts are the Seafood Creole, a melange of vegetables, shrimp, scallops, catfish, and mussels served with white rice and okra, and the chicken dishes (fried, smothered, or spicy honey), served with greens, okra, macaroni and cheese, potato salad, or yams. Meat entrees include Filet Mignon with String Beans and Home Fried Potatoes, Curry Lamb with Collard Greens and White Rice, and Baked Ham in Orange, Raisin, and Red Wine Sauce with Zucchini and Yams. Desserts are just as tantalizing, and include such treats as Southern Pecan Pie with Whipped Cream, coconut-flecked Sweet Potato Pie, and a Chocolate Pecan Brownie with Ice Cream and Hot Fudge.

Open seven days a week. American Express accepted.

B. Smith's
320 West 46th Street (between Eighth
   and Ninth Avenues)
(212) 315-1100

Former fashion model and television host Barbara Smith is the proprietor of this theater district Euro-style restaurant. The bar is a hangout for the movers and shakers of the young black elite. Serving up an eclectic menu that caters to a variety of tastes, the appetizers include an array of seafood choices: Gulf Shrimp in a Sauce of Chardonnay, Garlic, and Herbs; Fried Oysters with Wasabi Soy Sauce; and Pan-Fried Lump Fin Crab Cake with Chile Mayonnaise. Entrees of meat, poultry, and pasta include Smothered Pork Chops with Fried Green Apples, Roasted Chicken Breast Rubbed with Herbs and Shallots with Beurre Blanc and Couscous Pilaf; and Vermicelli with Maine Lobster, Wilted Onion, Herbal Tomato Butter, and Mascarpone.

Open seven days a week for lunch and dinner; brunch served Sunday. Major credit cards accepted.

Shark Bar
307 Amsterdam Avenue (between West 74th
   and West 75th Streets)
(212) 874-8500
www.sharkbar.com

This Upper West Side restaurant is the happening place for Manhattan's black elite. Dinner patrons make their way through the throngs at the bar to the elevated dining area. Once seated, dinner choices are traditional, with a spin. Starters include Louisiana Deep-Fried Crab Cakes, Harlem-Style Chicken Wings with Spicy Sauce, and Soul Roll (a concoction of sauteed collard greens, rice and black-eyed peas in puff pastry served with country gravy). Grilled Atlantic Salmon with Citrus Butter and Blackened Boneless Chicken Breast with Pineapple Salsa are just two of the entrees. Side dishes include Mashed Potatoes, Candied Yams, Potato Salad, String Beans with Smoked Turkey, Collard Greens, and the ubiquitous Macaroni and Cheese.

Open seven days a week. Brunch is served Saturday and Sunday. Major credit cards accepted.

SUGAR BAR RESTAURANT AND LOUNGE
254 West 72nd Street (between Broadway
   and West End Avenue)
(212) 579-0222

Owned by the fabulously famous rhythm-and-blues songwriting-singing duo Nick Ashford and Valerie Simpson, this exotic Upper West Side restaurant transports guests to the African homeland. The huge, ornate metal door that empties into the beautifully appointed dining room is a work of art, as is everything in this lavishly designed restaurant—from the carved bar, to the thatched hut bathrooms, to the exquisite menu featuring appetizers of South African Spiced Shrimp over Spinach Mashed Potatoes.

Open for dinner Monday through Saturday; brunch served Sunday. Major credit cards accepted.

DALLAS BBQ
1255 Third Avenue (between East 72nd
   and East 73rd Streets)
(212) 772-9393

Rotisserie Chicken, Barbecue Spareribs, Fried Onion Loaf, Fried Chicken Wings, Fried Shrimp, Vegetable Tempura, and Texas-sized novelty drinks are just a few of the items on the menu of this busy, but informal, East Side restaurant. A great place for families, there is an array of sides to choose from, such as Baked Beans, Corn on the Cob, Texas-Style Chili, Homemade Coleslaw, and a choice of salads and soup. The inexpensive yet hearty meals keep customers coming back. The early bird special offers two full meals of Chicken Soup, Rotisseried Half Chicken, and a choice of Baked or French-Fried Potatoes at a very reasonable price; it is available from noon to 6:30 P.M. during the week, and from noon to 5 P.M. on the weekends.

Open seven days a week. Other Dallas BBQ locations: 27 West 72nd Street, (212) 873-2004; 132 West 43rd Street, (212) 221-9000; 21 University Place, (212) 674-4450; and 132 Second Avenue, (212) 777-5574.

Here are several other restaurants that may be of interest.

DAYO
103 Greenwich Avenue (at West 12th Street)
(212) 924-3161

Caribbean and Southern cuisine

ISLAND SPICE
402 West 44th Street (between Ninth
    and Tenth Avenues)
(212) 765-2995

Caribbean cuisine

NEGRIL
362 West 23rd Street (between Eighth
    and Ninth Avenues)
(212) 807-6411

Caribbean cuisine

LIVE MUSIC

In New York City you can hear music or dance to it every night of the week. Club listings can be found in a variety of weekly magazines and newspapers, including *New York* magazine, *Time Out*

New York, and the *Village Voice,* to name a few. Or you can access information from the Web at www.sidewalk.com or www. newyork.citysearch.com.

BLUE NOTE
131 West 3rd Street (between MacDougal Street
   and Sixth Avenue)
(212) 475-8592
www.bluenote.net

Many of the greats have performed and continue to perform at this popular jazz and blues spot, including Natalie Cole with her uncle Freddie Cole (Nat's brother), Abbey Lincoln, the Frank Foster Band, and James Moody. If the cover and minimum are too steep at the tables, opt for standing room at the bar. This intimate club for jazz maniacs also hosts jam sessions into the wee hours of the morning.

Open seven days a week. Showtimes at 9:00 P.M. and 11:30 P.M. Cover charge begins at $40 per person with a $5 food/drink minimum at tables or $20 per person with a one drink minimum at the bar. Reservations suggested. For a performance schedule, call the club or visit their website.

BOTTOM LINE
15 West 4th Street (at Mercer Street)
(212) 228-6300

This funky, no-frills club is where Miles Davis, George Benson, and a host of other musicians have performed. It offers an eclectic mix of music—jazz, rock, blues, gospel, and world. If you're hungry, the Bottom Line serves bar food, including chips and salsa, burgers, pizza, and fries.

Open seven days a week. Cover charge is less than $20. Call for a performance schedule.

S.O.B.'s (SOUNDS OF BRAZIL)
204 Varick Street (at West Houston Street)
(212) 243-4940
www.sobs.com

This hot and happening club features live jazz and music from Africa, Cuba, Brazil, and the Caribbean. The soul and nouvelle cuisine menu offers dishes with Latin, Brazilian, and Caribbean influences. Monday nights starting at 7 P.M., patrons can dance to the rhythms of Latin orchestras, and free dance lessons are available.

Open Monday to Saturday from 6:30 P.M. Cover charge varies depending on artist; drink minimum is $15 per person at table. Major credit cards accepted. Reservations recommended. For a performance schedule, visit their Web site.

VILLAGE VANGUARD
178 Seventh Avenue (between 11th and Perry Streets)
(212) 255-4037

A historic jazz club in Greenwich Village, this is where the legendary pillars of jazz have played. John Coltrane, Dexter Gordon, Rahsaan Roland Kirk, Miles Davis, Thelonious Monk, and McCoy Tyner have all graced this tiny basement stage.

Open seven days a week. Showtimes at 9:30 P.M. and 11:30 P.M. Cover charge is $25 per person Monday through Friday, $30 per person on the weekends. Call for a performance schedule.

LOLA
30 West 22nd Street (between Fifth and Sixth Avenues)
(212) 675-6700

This swanky soul food restaurant hosts live music nightly. Monday and Sunday features jazz; Tuesday through Saturday, Caribbean, salsa, rhythm and blues, funk, and soul. There is a $20 minimum at the lounge tables. Showtimes at around 7:30 P.M. On Sunday enjoy the gospel brunch with seatings at 10:00 A.M., noon, and 2:00 P.M. Major credit cards accepted. Call for a performance schedule. (See page 50.)

THE JAZZ STANDARD
116 East 27th Street (between Park
    and Lexington Avenues)
(212) 576-2232

This sophisticated East Side basement club may take itself a little too seriously for some jazz buffs. But they do have great talent coming through, and it's intimate so you can really get into the performance.

Open Tuesday through Sunday. Tuesday through Thursday showtimes are at 8:00 P.M. and 10:00 P.M., with a cover charge of $18 and a $10 drink minimum per person. Friday and Saturday showtimes are at 8:00 P.M., 10:30 P.M., and 12:00 midnight, with a cover charge of $25 and a $10 drink minimum per person. Sunday showtimes are at 7:00 P.M. and 9:00 P.M., with a cover charge of $18 and a $10 drink minimum. Major credit cards accepted.

ROSELAND BALLROOM
239 West 52nd Street (between Broadway
    and Eighth Avenue)
(212) 247-0200

This historic ballroom is where big bands and ballroom dancers came to strut their stuff in the old days. Today one of the most popular events at the Ballroom is the monthly Oldies but Goodies Party, hosted by radio disc jockey Felix Hernandez. Folks come from the tri-state area and beyond to dance and relive their past to the music of the fifties, sixties, and seventies. In the lobby, encased in a display cabinet, are dance shoes once worn by Bill "Bojangles" Robinson and Broadway actor-hoofer Gregory Hines. Call for more information.

MORE MUSIC

IRIDIUM
Radisson Empire Hotel
48 West 63rd Street (between Broadway
   and Columbus Avenue)
(212) 582-2121
www.iridiumjazz.com

Open Monday through Saturday. Call for a performance schedule.

BIRDLAND
315 West 44th Street (between Eighth and Ninth
   Avenues)
(212) 581-3080

Open seven days a week. Call for a performance schedule.

SHOPPING

MACY'S HERALD SQUARE
The Blackberry Shop
151 West 34th Street (at Broadway)
(212) 695-4400

This boutique within Macy's sells Afrocentric art and artifacts, crafts, books, home furnishings, and accessories. Often the scene of book signings by black authors, the shop is a place where African American entrepreneurs promote their products.

Open seven days a week: Tuesday through Saturday from 10:00 A.M. to 8:30 P.M. and from 10:00 A.M. to 7:00 P.M. on Sunday.

PHAT FARM
129 Prince Street (between West Broadway
  and Wooster Street)
(212) 533-7428

This flagship clothing store of hip-hop impressario Russell Simmons's retail empire sells jeans, shirts, sweaters, T-shirts, and caps with "Classic American Flava."

Open Monday through Saturday from 11:00 A.M. to 7:00 P.M.; Sundays, from 12:00 noon to 6:00 P.M.

ASHANTI/LARGE SIZES
872 Lexington Avenue (between 65th and 66th Streets)
(212) 535-0740

The clothing at this store is geared toward plus-size women, and features sizes from 14 to 28+. Designed and manufactured in-house out of natural fabrics, many of the unique garments and accessories are created by up-and-coming designers.

Open Monday through Saturday.

TOURS OF MANHATTAN

The following companies offer tours of Manhattan that highlight some interesting African American heritage sites.

BIG ONION WALKING TOURS
(212) 439-1090

Central Park Tour
www.bigonion.com

Big Onion's Central Park walking tour explores the park's history and its design by Frederick Law Olmsted and Calvert Vaux. Stops include Seneca Village, an early black settlement in Manhattan in the 1800s, the site of the rocking chair riot, Strawberry Fields, and the Ramble. Call for meeting place, schedule, and prices.

Joyce Gold History Tours of New York
The Colonial Settlers of Wall Street Tour
(212) 242-5762
www.nyctours.com

This walking tour starts at old Trinity Church, right at the top of Wall Street by the New York Stock Exchange. In colonial times, blacks were allowed to worship at Trinity Church, but had to sit apart from the rest of the congregation. Fed up with being segregated, a group of black parishioners started their own church, St. Philips Episcopal Church on Centre Street, which is now located in Harlem. Some of the other sites covered in this tour of old New Amsterdam include the African Burial Ground between Duane and Reade Streets, the Five Points District (the site of present-day City Hall), and Fraunces Tavern on Pearl Street. Call for meeting place, schedule, and prices.

HARLEM

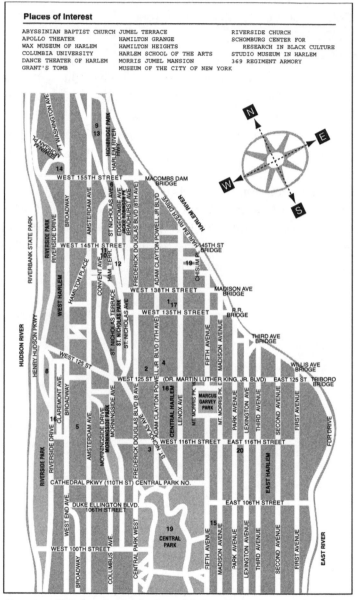

Courtesy of Harlem Spirituals, Gospel & Jazz Tours, Inc.

2

Harlem

HARLEM TODAY

Despite some hard times, Harlem is a thriving, bustling community that continues to celebrate its rich cultural history. Harlem is currently experiencing another Renaissance, one that echoes the building frenzy of the 1900s, when the community first began, and the cultural renaissance of the 1920s.

With its federal and state designation as an Empowerment Zone, money is being pumped into Harlem to improve existing businesses, renovate and build housing, and create jobs. Construction of new buildings to house retail stores and entertainment complexes signal a return of essential services to the community. Pathmark supermarket opened a twenty-four-hour store with rooftop parking on 125th Street and Lexington Avenue in April 1999, and in May 1999, ex-NBA player Magic Johnson cut the ribbon at the grand opening of his Starbucks Coffee at 125th Street and Adam Clayton Powell Jr. Boulevard. There is also a proposal to construct a $24 million, ten- to twelve-screen multiplex theater on Lexington Avenue, across from the new Pathmark. And the old Washburn Wire Factory at 115th Street in East Harlem is the future home of warehouse giants Home Depot and Price

Costco. In addition, Harlem USA, a 275,000-square-foot mall on the corner of Frederick Douglass Boulevard and 125th Street opened in time for holiday shoppers in December 1999. The $65 million complex houses The Disney Store, the nine-screen Magic Johnson Theatres, HMV Records, Old Navy, Modell's Sporting Goods, New York Sports Clubs, and the Chase Manhattan Bank. Harlem's rebirth is attracting all kinds of people, including former president Bill Clinton, who plans to set up his office in the heart of Harlem on West 125th Street.

The retail boom is not the only excitement going on in the Harlem community. The music is back and it is everywhere. Clubs and restaurants are featuring live music, including swing orchestras and jazz combos, open-mic nights for singers and spoken word artists, and weekend gospel brunches. Showmans at 375 West 125th Street, St. Nick's Pub at 773 St. Nicholas Avenue, and the Cotton Club at 656 West 125th Street are just a few of the clubs offering live music.

Cultural arts institutions in Harlem are also participating in the renaissance. Nine cultural centers—Aaron Davis Hall, The Apollo Theatre Foundation, Inc., the Boys Choir of Harlem, Inc., Dance Theatre of Harlem, Harlem School of the Arts, Inc., Jazzmobile, Inc., National Black Theatre, Inc., Schomburg Center for Research in Black Culture, and The Studio Museum in Harlem—have organized into the Harlem Strategic Cultural Collaborative. Their mission is to collaborate on tourism promotion, audience development, and public school outreach.

As Harlem continues its metamorphosis from a neglected, crime-ridden community to a thriving, productive center of culture and diversity, the people and events that have made Harlem the heart of the African American's story in New York will endure.

HARLEM ITINERARY

Harlem is hot. The new Renaissance is in full swing, and buses are jam-packed with tourists who are flocking to the many cultural and heritage sites, restaurants, and nightclubs. Visitors from Japan,

France, and the United States are learning about the rich history of America's most famous black community. Evidence of the revival is on every block. New construction, restorations, and renovations abound. Basketball legend Magic Johnson and animation conglomerate Disney are part of a huge economic movement that have brought a variety of retail outlets and basic services back to the community, including multi-screen movie houses, Starbucks Coffee, and The Disney Store. Because there is so much to see and do, a visitor needs a plan in order to get the full effect of this incredible neighborhood.

A tour of Harlem can happen a number of different ways. Here are several options.

- An escorted walking or bus tour to historic sites and landmarks followed by a scrumptious meal at a local soul food restaurant.

- An evening of jazz at several of Harlem's jumping joints, or a trip to the world famous Apollo Theatre to witness the birth of a star at the legendary Wednesday "Amateur Night at the Apollo."

- A Sunday-morning tour of historic churches with a rousing sermon and inspirational singing, or a hand-clapping, foot-stomping gospel brunch at a neighborhood restaurant.

▼▼

RENAMING OF THE AVENUES OF HARLEM

Some of the major avenues of Harlem have been renamed after prominent black figures. Here is a key to help you navigate the terrain, since some people still refer to these streets by their original names.

NOW	THEN
Malcolm X Boulevard	Lenox Avenue
Adam Clayton Powell Jr. Boulevard	Seventh Avenue
Frederick Douglass Boulevard	Eighth Avenue

▲▲▲

If you have time, try to do it all! It's well worth it.

If you decide to do Harlem on your own, the intersection of 125th Street and Adam Clayton Powell Jr. Boulevard is the perfect starting point. The Apollo Theatre at 253 West 125th Street offers tours by appointment; The Studio Museum in Harlem, 144 West 125th Street, provides an artistic window into black culture; and Sylvia's, the famous soul food restaurant at 328 Adam Clayton Powell Jr. Boulevard and 126th Street, will titillate your taste buds with its "down-home" offerings (open for breakfast, lunch, and dinner). Vegetarians can fortify themselves with a wide selection of juices and vegetarian dishes at the Uptown Juice Bar, located at 54 West 125th Street, and coffee lovers can stop for an espresso or double café latte at Magic Johnson's Starbucks at 77 West 125th Street. The Mount Morris Historic District, between West 118th Street and West 124th Street, is right around the corner with its breathtaking examples of historic brownstones built during the late 1800s when the elevated trains reached Harlem. Also in the neighborhood are Marcus Garvey Park and the Mount Morris Park Watch Tower.

Farther up Adam Clayton Powell Jr. Boulevard, at number 2247, is Wells Supper Club, a neighborhood institution since 1938. Closed for renovations, the restaurant was known for its world-famous chicken and waffles, a Harlem delicacy. On 135th Street, between Adam Clayton Powell Jr. Boulevard and Malcolm X Boulevard, is the Harlem YMCA, at 180 West 135th Street, where poets Claude McKay and Langston Hughes and baseball legend Jackie Robinson lived. Just up the street, on the corner of Malcolm X Boulevard, is the Schomburg Center for Research in Black Culture: A visit to its art gallery and gift shop is a must. Between Adam Clayton Powell Jr. Boulevard and Frederick Douglass Boulevard, on 138th Street and 139th Street, are the King Model Houses, also known as Striver's Row. These historic blocks are examples of some of the best architecture in New York City, and were home to many famous black entertainers during the Harlem Renaissance. As you round the corner of the Striver's Row District to Frederick Douglass Boulevard heading north, Londel's (at 2620 Frederick Douglass Boulevard), a sophisticated eating establishment with a menu to match, is on the east side of the street. The Southern-inspired dishes are delicious, and a soak in the ambience of this lovely dining room is a perfect way to refresh yourself before embarking on the rest of your Harlem tour. On the west side of the boulevard at 2611 is the Sugar Shack, a neighborhood hangout where you can eat and drink with the locals while enjoying open-mic performances or networking opportunities.

Hamilton Heights (West 140th Street to West 145th Street, between Amsterdam and St. Nicholas Avenues) is where Alexander Hamilton's home, Hamilton Grange, and City College are located. The Audubon Terrace Historic District (West 155th Street and West 156th Street, between Broadway and Riverside Drive) is the site of eight historic Italian Renaissance research buildings and the Audubon Ballroom site where Malcolm X was assassinated. Jumel Terrace Historic District (West 160th Street to West 162nd Street, between Edgecombe and St. Nicholas Avenues) is the location of the clapboard houses of Sylvan Terrace, the Morris-Jumel Mansion, and the well-tended brownstones of Sugar Hill. For a more in-depth look at the historic neighborhoods of Harlem, you can book an excursion offered by a tour operator. (See page 140.)

HISTORIC SITES AND LANDMARKS

AUDUBON BALLROOM SITE
3940 Broadway (at West 165th Street)

The ballroom is the site of the assassination of civil rights activist Malcolm X on February 21, 1965. Malcolm was speaking at a rally by his recently formed group, the Organization for Afro-American

Audubon Ballroom Site, at West 165th Street and Broadway (Photo by Linda Tarrant-Reid)

Unity, when he was killed. The Audubon Building has since been renovated and now houses several restaurants, a bookstore, and a bank on the street level. The ballroom is being restored, and plans for a memorial and a museum commemorating the life of the slain activist are being planned. An inscription over the doorway of the entrance to the lobby reads: "Knowledge 5.19.25 El-Hajj Malik El-Shabazz 2.21.65 Courage." The dates denote Malcolm X's birth and death. Not open to the public.

To learn more about the life of this great black nationalist leader, read *The Autobiography of Malcolm X,* co-written with Alex Haley (1964) or *Seventh Child,* by Malcolm's nephew Rodnell P. Collins, with A. Peter Bailey (1998).

JUMEL TERRACE HISTORIC DISTRICT
West 160th Street to West 162nd Street (between
  Edgecombe and St. Nicholas Avenues)

This neighborhood is a spectacular display of nineteenth-century row houses built of limestone, brownstone, and brick. The brightly painted clapboard houses on the narrow Sylvan Terrace were built in 1882. African American singer-actor-and-activist Paul Robeson lived in a row house located around the corner, at 16 Jumel Terrace, from the 1950s until 1967. The Morris-Jumel Mansion, George Washington's headquarters during the Battle of Harlem Heights, is also located on this street. (See page 95.)

AUDUBON TERRACE HISTORIC DISTRICT
Broadway (between West 155th and 156th Streets)

Audubon Terrace, a complex of elegant buildings, was conceived as a research center outside of the university setting by millionaire philanthropist Archer M. Huntington. The eight Italian Renaissance buildings, mostly designed by Archer's cousin Charles P. Huntington, were built between 1907 and 1930 on sections of the former estate of John James Audubon that Huntington purchased. The buildings house the Hispanic Society, the former offices of the American Geographical Society, the Church of Our Lady of Esperanza, the American Academy of Arts and Letters, and the National Institute of Arts and Letters.

GRAVEYARD OF AMERICAN NATIONAL HEROES
West 153rd to West 155th Streets (between Amsterdam
  Avenue and Riverside Drive)

One of the oldest cemeteries in Manhattan, the graveyard is owned by Trinity Church in lower Manhattan. Some of the famous

Sylvan Terrace, West 162nd Street and St. Nicholas
Avenue (Photo by Linda Tarrant-Reid)

people buried here include conservationist John Audubon, founder
of the Audubon Society, Eliza Jumel, mistress of Morris-Jumel
Mansion, and Clement Clark Moore, author of "'Twas the Night
Before Christmas."

HAMILTON HEIGHTS HISTORIC DISTRICT
West 140th Street to West 145th Street (between
   Amsterdam and St. Nicholas Avenues)

This historic residential community was part of the famed Sugar
Hill section of Harlem, where middle-class blacks lived in the

1920s. Among the early African American residents were artists, writers, and musicians. The tree-lined streets of brownstone and limestone row houses built between 1895 and 1902 were formerly part of Alexander Hamilton's estate, Hamilton Grange.

369TH REGIMENT ARMORY
2366 Fifth Avenue (between 142nd and 143rd Streets)
(212) 281-3308

Home to the 369th Veterans Association, this armory is named for the Harlem Hellfighters, the all-black regiment that served in World War I. Not recognized by the United States government as part of the military, the regiment, which was originally the 15th Regiment of the New York National Guards, fought on the front lines in Germany alongside French troops because the United States Army did not allow blacks in combat. The unit was awarded the croix de guerre for heroism and the Legion of Honor by the French government. The museum has displays and photographs documenting the participation of black soldiers in combat from World War I to the present. Call for museum hours.

HAMILTON GRANGE NATIONAL MEMORIAL
287 Convent Avenue (between 141st and 142nd Streets)
(212) 283-5154

Hamilton Grange, built in 1801, was the summer home of Alexander Hamilton (1755–1804), first Secretary of the Treasury of the United States, author of the Federalist Papers, and founder of the *New York Evening Post* newspaper. Hamilton lived in his federal-style home for only two years (1802–1804), before dying from wounds suffered in a duel with his longtime adversary, Aaron Burr. The Grange was moved to 287 Convent Avenue from its original site when a developer purchased the land in 1879. The house was donated to St. Luke's Church and served as its chapel until a new church was built next door to the house. The Grange was closed in 1992 for safety reasons after an engineering analysis found severe

Hamilton Grange, Convent Avenue between West 141st and West 142nd Streets
(Photo by Linda Tarrant-Reid)

structural damage. Visitors can view the outside of the Grange and get an idea of what a nineteenth-century country estate looked like. (Call for more information.)

ABYSSINIAN BAPTIST CHURCH
132 West 138th Street (between Malcolm X
and Adam Clayton Powell Jr. Boulevards)

This famous church, founded by Thomas Paul in 1808, was the first independent Baptist church in New York. Congressman and civil rights activist Adam Clayton Powell Jr. and his father, Adam Clayton Sr., were both pastors here. With its tradition of community involvement and political activism, Abyssinian has long been a fulcrum of the Harlem community. Currently pastored by Rev. Calvin Butts, the church is involved in the revitalization of Harlem through the Abyssinian Development Corporation, which purchases, renovates, and sells buildings in the community. Rev. Calvin Butts, a community activist in his own right, has received a lot of media attention for his ongoing feud with New York City Mayor Rudolph Giuliani. The church has a small museum consisting of artifacts and memorabilia that is dedicated to the life and work of Adam Clayton Powell Jr.

MOTHER A.M.E. ZION CHURCH
140-146 West 137th Street (between Malcolm X
and Adam Clayton Powell Jr. Boulevards)

Established in 1796, the church is the oldest African Methodist church in New York State. It was founded in lower Manhattan by

Mother A.M.E. Zion Church, West 137th Street between Malcolm X and Adam Clayton Powell Jr. Boulevards (Photo by Linda Tarrant-Reid)

James Varick, Abraham Thompson, ex-slave Peter Williams, who was a sexton at the John Street Methodist Church, and others after they suffered discrimination while worshipping with the white congregation of John Street Methodist Church. The church was originally located in a house on Cross Street and in 1800 the congregation moved to a newly built church at the corner of Church and Leonard Streets. Mother A.M.E. Zion has a rich history and played a key role in New York City's Underground Railroad by providing shelter for fugitive slaves fleeing to Canada. The church was also the site of mass-meetings protesting the Fugitive Slave Law of 1850. The spiritual home to many famous historic black figures including Sojourner Truth, Frederick Douglass, Harriet Tubman, and Paul Robeson, the church continues to uphold its tradition of outreach and activism.

CITY COLLEGE OF NEW YORK (CCNY)
West 138th to West 140th Streets (between Amsterdam Avenue and St. Nicholas Terrace)

This gothic structure high upon the hill was founded in 1847 and is part of the network of colleges, along with Brooklyn College and Queens College, that comprise the City University of New York. The four-year college is situated on thirty-five acres in the St. Nicholas Heights section of Harlem. The college is the alma mater of many successful black New Yorkers, such as former chairman of the Joint Chiefs of Staff and current Secretary of State Colin Powell, writer Walter Mosley, businessman Bruce Llewelyn, and writer-artist Faith Ringgold. The school's performing arts center, Aaron Davis Hall, is a major venue for performing arts events.

ST. NICHOLAS HISTORIC DISTRICT (STRIVER'S ROW)
West 138th Street and West 139th Street (between Adam Clayton Powell Jr. and Frederick Douglass Boulevards)

The beautiful nineteenth-century row houses here were built by developer David H. King Jr., and were designed for wealthy New

Striver's Row, between West 137th and West 139th Streets, and Adam Clayton Powell Jr. and Frederick Douglass Boulevards (Photos by Linda Tarrant-Reid)

Yorkers in 1891 by the architectural firms of James Brown Lord, Bruce Price, and Clarence S. Luce, and McKim, Mead, and White. During the Harlem Renaissance in the 1920s and 1930s, notables such as composer-musician Eubie Blake, bandleader Noble Sissle, musician W. C. Handy, and composer Will Marion Cook lived in these stately homes. Blake and Sissle wrote the music for the successful black Broadway show *Shuffle Along* in 1921 (see page 44).

Harlem YMCA

180 West 135th Street (between Malcolm X
  and Adam Clayton Powell Jr. Boulevards)
(212) 281-4100

This YMCA was one of two "colored" Ys in New York City, and became the home away from home to many African American men who migrated from the South and the Caribbean to Manhattan in

Harlem YMCA on West 135th Street between Adam Clayton Powell
Jr. and Malcolm X Boulevards (Photo by Linda Tarrant-Reid)

the early 1900s. The first Colored Men's Branch of the YMCA
opened in 1901 in a storefront at 132 West 53rd Street, which was
known as Black Broadway. In 1903 the New York YMCA purchased
two buildings and moved the Colored Men's Branch to 245-252
West 53rd Street. The West 135th Street branch was opened in
1919. The YMCA offered recent arrivals a place to stay, listen to
lectures, enjoy theatrical productions, and take classes.

Writer and poet of the Harlem Renaissance Claude McKay lived
in the Harlem YMCA from 1941 to 1946. McKay was the author of

the moving poem "If We Must Die," a reference to the black soldiers who fought in WWI yet still faced prejudice after they returned from war. McKay's first novel, *Home to Harlem,* was considered a controversial and racy depiction of Harlem life. His collection of poems entitled *Harlem: Negro Metropolis* was published in 1940.

The Harlem Y was also the home of Harlem Renaissance poet-writer Langston Hughes, composer-arranger Billy Strayhorn, and many others. Actors Sidney Poitier, Eartha Kitt, and Vinnette Carol were active in the Y's Little Theater.

JAMES WELDON JOHNSON HOUSE
187 West 135TH Street (between Malcolm X and Adam
  Clayton Powell Jr. Boulevards)

Lawyer, educator, poet, lyricist, composer, and writer James Weldon Johnson (1871–1938) lived in this house from 1925 to 1938. While working as principal in a Jacksonville, Florida, high school, Johnson wrote the words to the Negro Anthem "Lift Every Voice and Sing" to commemorate Abraham Lincoln's birthday. He was the first black man admitted to the Florida Bar. In 1906 he served as United States consul in Venezuela, and in 1909 he was appointed head of the U.S. Consulate in Nicaragua. An early organizer for the NAACP, Johnson became the organization's first black president in 1920. The author of *The Autobiography of an Ex-Colored Man* (1912) and *Black Manhattan* (1930), Johnson collaborated with his brother, composer John Rosamond Johnson, on over 200 musical compositions. The James Weldon Johnson house is now a private residence.

ST. PHILIP'S EPISCOPAL CHURCH
204 West 134th Street (between Adam Clayton Powell Jr.
  and Frederick Douglass Boulevards)
(212) 862-4940

The church was established in 1818 by black congregants of Trinity Episcopal Church in lower Manhattan, who could no longer tolerate being segregated from white parishioners during worship service (see page 26). The black parishioners held their own services in a "colored public school" on William Street until 1812, then moved to a room over a carpenter's shop on Cliff Street between Perry (now Peck's Slip) and Beekman Streets. The congregation's next move was to Rose Street near Pearl Street, and in 1818 they relocated to a framed church on Collect Street (now Centre Street) between Anthony (now Worth) and Leonard Streets. After moving to several more locations in lower Manhattan—on Broadway, Mulberry Street, and West 25th Street—the church finally settled into its present location in Harlem in 1910. African American architect Vertner Tandy, who also designed hair-care titan Madame C. J. Walker's estate, Villa Lewaro, in Irvington-on-the-Hudson, New York (see page 194) was commissioned to design St. Philip's in Harlem.

Astor Row Houses
8–62 West 130th Street (between Malcolm X Boulevard and Fifth Avenue)

Charles Buek designed these impressive brick row houses with wooden porches, which were built between 1880 and 1883 by developer William Astor. Astor built many other apartment buildings and row houses in Harlem, as well, in the early 1880s. Currently, the Abyssinian Development Corporation and the New York Landmarks Conservancy are restoring these houses.

Hotel Theresa
2090 Adam Clayton Powell Jr. Boulevard (at 125th Street)

Now an office building, the Hotel Theresa, which was built in 1913 by white cigar maker Gustav Seidenberg, became Harlem's premiere hotel for black folks starting in 1940 as the downtown hotels were closed to blacks at the time. *Ebony* magazine, in a 1946 article, compared the Theresa to the Waldorf-Astoria, the elite white establishment on Park Avenue. Popular with celebrities of the day, the hotel was "Brown Bomber" Joe Louis's home and headquarters at the height of his boxing career. The Theresa's bar was the information center of the black community and the base of operations for two of Harlem's most famous reporters, Billy Rowe and Dan Burley. Located close to the historic Apollo Theatre, many of the entertainers who headlined at the Apollo stayed at this classy establishment or patronized the bar, including Dizzy Gillespie, Count Basie, Lena Horne, and Duke Ellington.

In 1960 Cuban president Fidel Castro came to New York City to address the United Nations. When he became disenchanted with the service at his midtown hotel, Castro and his entourage of forty moved to the Theresa Hotel in Harlem. During Castro's stay at the hotel, he hosted visits by Russian Premier Nikita Khrushchev, poet-author Langston Hughes, poet Allen Ginsburg, and Malcolm X. The Theresa is now a monument to its historic past.

APOLLO THEATRE

253 West 125th Street (between Frederick Douglass and
   Adam Clayton Powell Jr. Boulevards)
(212) 531-5305

This bastion of black entertainment was originally called the Seamon and Hurtig Music Hall, but was renamed the Apollo by its new owner in 1934. From bebop to blues, to rock and roll, to jazz, to hip-hop, and rhythm and blues, this music mecca has presented great entertainers like Billie Holiday, Sarah Vaughn, Cab Calloway, Duke Ellington, Stevie Wonder, the Temptations, Diana Ross and the Supremes, and Gladys Knight and the Pips. The renowned *Amateur Night at the Apollo*, at which, in the old days, the untalented got the hook, is still a favorite every Wednesday at 7:30 P.M. Watch young talent as they brave their jitters and reach for that star.

Tours available. Call for more information and performance schedule. (See sidebar, page 80.)

THE APOLLO THEATRE

This world-famous theater opened in 1913 as the Seamon and Hurtig Music Hall, a burlesque theater that featured vaudeville acts. One-hundred twenty-fifth Street was the center of a largely white community and many of the businesses only catered to a white clientele. Blacks moving to Harlem from the Tenderloin and San Juan Hill could not frequent the Apollo or the Theresa Hotel at that time.

During the Great Depression, the music hall fell on hard times and was sold to Sidney Cohen in 1933. Cohen reopened the theater in 1934 as the Apollo, with a film screening and performances by the Benny Carter Orchestra. As the country began its slow recovery from the Depression, a new era began to dawn in Harlem. The program format at the Apollo was enhanced by the arrival of Frank Schiffman, who directed the lavish stage revues hosted by legendary emcee Ralph Cooper. During Harlem's golden age of music in the thirties and forties, the 1,600-seat auditorium hosted thirty shows a week that were broadcast live on radio. Artists performed in front of the Apollo's outrageous patrons, dubbed by some "the toughest audience in show business." All the greats performed at the Apollo: Lionel Hampton, Cab Calloway, Duke Ellington, Ella Fitzgerald, Count Basie, Lena Horne, Pearl Bailey, and Sarah Vaughn, to name a few. Thelonious Monk, Louis Armstrong, and Charlie Parker were also regulars.

In the fifties, the Apollo and the surrounding community experienced a decline. But the Apollo was brought back to life in the sixties with the birth of rock and roll. Chubby Checker performed his hit song "Let's Do the Twist" there, and Smokey Robinson and the Miracles and the entire Motown stable all made appearances at this landmark music hall.

By the 1970s the Apollo had lost its lustre. Many of the talented black musicians and performers began appearing at venues that had been previously closed to them, and their gig fees escalated.

Apollo Theatre, 253 West 125th Street, between
Frederick Douglass and Adam Clayton Powell Jr.
Boulevards (Photo by Linda Tarrant-Reid)

Unable to pay the performers their going rate, the Apollo closed
its doors in 1977. In 1981 former Manhattan borough president
Percy Sutton and a group of investors purchased the old theater for
$225,000, and started up the famous Wednesday *Amateur Night at
the Apollo*. With the help of a $20 million renovation, and the pub-
licity from the TV program *It's Showtime at the Apollo*, which featured the best acts of amateur night, the theater regained its
footing. Nevertheless, management problems and inconsistent
bookings have prevented the landmark from fully reliving its glorious
past. Today the Apollo stands at the nexus of the new Harlem
Renaissance as it awaits yet another rebirth into the new millennium.

Mount Morris Historic District
West 118th to West 124th Streets (between Mount Morris Park West and Malcolm X Boulevard)

Mount Morris, one of the oldest neighborhoods in Harlem, was created in the early 1880s after the opening of the elevated trains. The magnificent brownstones fronting Marcus Garvey Park (formerly Mount Morris Park) and on the streets west of the park have gone through many changes over the years, starting out as single-family homes and later evolving into multi-family dwellings. With the revitalization of the Harlem business community, and the gentrification of the neighborhoods, many of these houses are now being renovated and restored.

Marcus Garvey Park
East 124th Street (between Mount Morris Park West and Malcolm X Boulevard)

Formerly known as Mount Morris Park, this park was renamed for the Jamaican political activist Marcus Garvey (1887–1940), the father of Pan-Africanism or the "Back to Africa Movement," which promoted the migration of blacks to Africa to escape oppression in the U.S. Through his travels, Garvey became acutely aware of the injustices suffered by blacks, and decided to form an organization whose goal was to uplift black people. He founded the Universal Negro Improvement Association (UNIA) on the island of Jamaica in 1914. Garvey came to Harlem in 1916 and quickly solidified his position as a black leader. In 1918 he published the *Negro World*, a newspaper, in which many of his speeches appeared. In 1920 the UNIA held an international convention that attracted over 25,000 delegates to Harlem. Garvey's success was short-lived after the failure of his shipping company, the Black Star Line, which he founded to employ blacks in the shipping industry and to transport blacks back to their African homeland. In 1925 he was convicted of mail fraud and spent two years in prison. Garvey was deported to his home in Jamaica in 1927.

Mount Morris Park Watch Tower
East 122nd Street (located in Marcus Garvey Park)

Located in the middle of Marcus Garvey Park, the octagonal cast-iron bell tower was built in 1856 to alert the surrounding community to fire. The tower became obsolete when fire alarm boxes were installed around New York City in 1878.

Langston Hughes House
20 East 127th Street (between Fifth and Madison
  Avenues)

Harlem Renaissance author-poet Langston Hughes (1902–1967) lived in an apartment in this three-story brownstone during the last twenty years of his life. Hughes, a prolific traveler and writer, chronicled life around him whether he was in Harlem, Washington, D.C., California, Mexico, Europe, or Cuba. He wrote poetry, fiction, plays, children's books, humor, and biographies. Hughes's first collection of poetry, entitled *The Weary Blues* (1926), described the music being played in Harlem in the early 1920s using the cadences of black speech and the music's rhythm. In his 1940 autobiography, *The Big Sea,* Hughes chronicled his life up to 1931, including a vivid account of the Harlem Renaissance. In the poem "Harlem" (published in his 1951 collection of poems entitled *Montage of a Dream Deferred*), Hughes posed the widely recognized question, "What happens to a dream deferred?" in response to the changes he had witnessed in Harlem. The Langston Hughes house is now a private residence.

Columbia University
West 114th to 120th Streets (between Broadway and
  Amsterdam Avenue)

Designed in Italian Renaissance style by the architectural firm of McKim, Mead, and White in the 1890s, the famous university was made to resemble an urban academic village. Its centerpiece is Low Memorial Library, a classical Roman building with Grecian detail. The expanding university moved here from its downtown location at 49th Street and Madison Avenue in 1897.

Some of the celebrated African Americans who attended the university include Renaissance poet-writer Langston Hughes, who attended Columbia College for one year, and civil rights activist-actor-opera singer Paul Robeson, who graduated from the law school. African American psychologist Alvin Poussaint also attended the university.

WASHINGTON AND LAFAYETTE
114th Street and Morningside Avenue

French artist Frédéric Auguste Bartholdi sculpted this statue of generals George Washington and Marquis De Lafayette shaking hands. Installed at the intersection of 114th Street and Morningside Avenue, adjacent to Morningside Park, the statue was a gift from Charles B. Rouss to the City of New York on April 19, 1900. Bartholdi also sculpted the Statue of Liberty in New York Harbor.

THE CATHEDRAL OF ST. JOHN THE DIVINE
1047 Amsterdam Avenue (at West 112th Street)
(212) 316-7540
www.stjohndivine.org

This majestic cathedral, reportedly the world's largest, is unofficially dubbed St. John the Unfinished. Although construction began in 1892, the church has yet to be completed. The cathedral site is on a thirteen-acre plot that includes a garden with over one hundred plant species. The sanctuary, which seats 2,500, can hold up to 4,000 and is the length of two football fields. The principal church of the Episcopal Diocese of New York, St. John the Divine has been the site of memorial services for many prominent members of the African American community. Its programs include Cathedral Community Cares, an outreach program, and Cathedral Arts, which sponsors cultural events at the church.

The Cathedral of St. John the Divine, Amsterdam Avenue at West 112th Street (Photo by Linda Tarrant-Reid)

The gift shop, open daily from 9 A.M. to 5 P.M., sells crafts and books.

DUKE ELLINGTON STATUE
East 110th Street and Fifth Avenue

The monument, designed by artist Robert Graham, portrays jazz composer and arranger Edward Kennedy "Duke" Ellington standing in front of a grand piano that is hoisted over the heads of sculpted ladies. Duke Ellington (1899–1974) was a prolific composer who created hundreds of works, including the masterful "Black, Brown, and Beige," "Mood Indigo," and "Black and Tan Fantasy." Known for his signature song "Take the A Train," written by Billy Strayhorn in 1939, Ellington, in his earlier career, was the bandleader for the world-renowned Cotton Club Band.

Duke Ellington Statue at Fifth Avenue and 110th
Street (Photo by Linda Tarrant-Reid)

FAMOUS ADDRESSES, FAMOUS PEOPLE

During the 1920s, 1930s, 1940s, and 1950s, Harlem was home to
many entertainers, educators, artists, writers, activists, and schol-
ars. It's really amazing to see, by address, how closely knit this
community was during its heyday. The following is just a sampling
of celebrity addresses in Harlem, some of which have been designated as national historic places.

PIG FOOT MARY'S STAND
West 135th and Lenox Avenue

Pig Foot Mary (a.k.a. Lillian Harris) was one of Harlem's most
famous success stories of the early 1900s. Mary began selling her

steamed pig feet, hog maws, and chitterlings from a baby carriage on West 60th Street, shortly after she arrived in New York around 1901. Pig Foot Mary moved her concession stand to the corner of 135th Street and Lenox Avenue in Harlem in 1917, where she sold her pork delicacies from a specially designed steam table. She met and married a Harlem newsstand owner. With the money Mary was raking in from her porcine business, she invested in Harlem real estate. By 1925, with her net worth estimated at $375,000, Mary retired and moved to Pasadena, California.

FLORENCE MILLS HOUSE
220 West 135th Street (between Adam Clayton Powell Jr. and Frederick Douglass Boulevards)

This was the home of actress-singer-dancer Florence Mills from 1910 to 1927. Mills starred in the Broadway smash hit *Shuffle Along* and the Harlem production of *Blackbirds*, which toured Europe for a year. Mills returned home from the tour critically ill and died weeks later at the age of 32. Her funeral was at Howell Undertaking Parlor on 137th Street and Seventh Avenue, where thousands came to say goodbye. The crowd that watched the cortege go by was estimated to be over 150,000.

WILL MARION COOK HOUSE
221 West 138th Street (between Adam Clayton Powell Jr. and Frederick Douglass Boulevards)

This three-story Georgian Revival brick town house on Striver's Row, built in 1891, was the home of African-American composer-musician-conductor Will Marion Cook (1869–1944) from 1918 until his death. Cook studied the violin with Joseph Joachim in Berlin and with Antonin Dvorak. Cook became frustrated pursuing his classical music career because of discrimination and turned to popular music. He collaborated with Bob Cole and Paul Laurence Dunbar on black Broadway shows, including *Clorindy* and *In Dahomey*. (See pages 44–45.)

DUNBAR APARTMENTS
2588 Adam Clayton Powell Jr. Boulevard (between 149th and 150th Streets)

Built between 1926 and 1928 by John D. Rockefeller, this apartment building was the first co-op for African Americans. Prominent residents included A. Philip Randolph, activist and founder of the Brotherhood of Sleeping Car Porters Union, dancer Bill "Bojangles" Robinson, and Matthew Henson, the first explorer to reach the North Pole. A plaque on the front of the building describes the famous former tenants.

THE BLACK WHITE HOUSE APARTMENT COMPLEX
409 Edgecombe Avenue (at 155th Street)

Referred to as the Black White House, this twelve-story apartment complex overlooking the Harlem River and the Macomb Dam Bridge is adjacent to the famed Polo Grounds (where the New York Giants, both baseball and football, and briefly the New York Mets, played their home games), now the Polo Grounds housing project.

This famous building was home to many prominent and powerful African Americans, including Supreme Court Justice Thurgood Marshall, NAACP president Roy Wilkins, artist Aaron Douglass, former NAACP president Walter White, and scholar-activist W. E. B. DuBois. Entertainers Cab Calloway and Fats Waller also called number 409 home. It is still a very imposing building, high on the hill overlooking the bridge with an unobstructed view of Yankee Stadium.

935 ST. NICHOLAS AVENUE (AT 155TH STREET)

This six-story, gothic-style apartment building was home to musician-composer Duke Ellington from 1939 to 1961. Composer Billy Strayhorn described Duke's apartment to his friends back home in Pittsburgh as all white, even the carpets. Duke lived in apartment 4A.

MARVIN SMITH, PHOTOGRAPHER

Marvin Smith, photographer (Photo by Linda Tarrant-Reid)

Marvin and Morgan Smith, twins from Lexington, Kentucky, arrived in Harlem in September 1933 after stopping in Cincinnati, Ohio, long enough to realize it wasn't for them. In Ohio, they hopped on a bus for New York City with newfound friend Horace Hicks. They were heading to New York to develop their skills as artists and photographers. Although raised in the South, the brothers had never really encountered overt racism, and it wasn't until they boarded the bus that racism reared its ugly head. "The bus driver told us to move to the back, we couldn't sit in the front of the bus," said Marvin Smith, the surviving twin, in a 1999 interview.

Undaunted, the three young men continued their journey determined to not let anything change their course. Upon arriving at the bus terminal in New York City, they were greeted by a huge billboard advertising the film *The Emperor Jones* starring Paul Robeson, certainly a sign of things to come. They were impressed by New York, not just the big city aspect but also that black people were so visible. "We ended up on Lenox Avenue in Harlem. We were really impressed with all the people, who were mostly black. There were black businesses—haberdasheries, restaurants, and bars on top of bars," reminisced Marvin.

The club scene was going strong in Harlem in the 1930s and there was lots of music to be heard. Marvin and Morgan Smith recounted:

A lot of white people frequented Harlem, because at that time the nightlife of New York City was in Harlem. The Cotton Club was a place where they went to see black performers. The Cotton Club was for white audiences only. I went to the Cotton Club to take pictures with my brother of the review. We usually took the pictures during rehearsals. The way they kept black people out of the Cotton Club was very subtle. For instance, if you came to the door they would say you did not have a reservation—it wasn't overt. Another establishment in Harlem that discriminated against black people was the Lowe Theater that was right across the street from the Hotel Theresa. They had black ushers, but I had to sit in the balcony. I couldn't sit on the first floor with the rest of the audience.

Marvin and Morgan Smith chronicled a very important time in Harlem's history. From their loft studio at 243 West 125th Street, located next door to the Apollo Theatre, they photographed the who's who in the world of black entertainment, politics, and business, including singer Lena Horne, Supreme Court Justice Thurgood Marshall, and entrepreneur Rose Morgan. They also documented the club scene: Ella Fitzgerald at the Savoy, the Cotton Club Chorus Line, and the Club Zanzibar Chorines.

Other popular nightclubs were Minton's Playhouse, the Hotcha, where Fats Waller played. That's where the picture was taken with him at the piano—the place on St. Nicholas Avenue that had singing waiters and waitresses. Lucky's was the name of the club—where Claudia McNeal waitressed. She went on to become an actress. There was the Lafayette Theater, there was Well's, and Count Basie's. And of course, Small's Paradise was the place to dance with continuous music by the bands of the day, like Chick Webb, Lucky Millinder, Fletcher Henderson, and Lionel Hampton. The Dorsey Brothers came up to Harlem and a number of white bands like Benny Goodman would come and listen and copy the style of music. We took pictures of most of the musicians I named.

My brother and I worked for the Works Progress Administration—the WPA*—it was a government project. They allowed you to work three days a week, five hours a day. Construction work, labor work. Working three days a week, we made more than we made in Kentucky working six days a week. We were very thrifty, we made $5 per day each. We lived at 2400 Seventh Avenue, that's the corner of 140th Street [northwest corner]—the building is still there. The building was next door to the Woodside Hotel at that time. Some musician has an album named *At the Woodside*. We were always being entertained by people walking down the street at 4 in the morning who were on their way to an after-hours place. It was a mixture of white and black people who were partying.

There was a place called Chez Clinton, Clinton Moore was the owner, that was at 135th [Street] and Seventh Avenue. It was a popular place. That was the place where Gloria Van-

*WPA—Works Progress Administration was a government program in which writers, artists, and other unemployed people were hired to work on projects such as writing books, painting murals, and landscaping public parks.

Mystery in Magic, a 1939 mural by WPA artist Charles Alston that currently hangs in Harlem Hospital. (From the Photographs and Prints Division, Schomburg Center for Research in Black Culture, The New York Public Library, Astor, Lenox, and Tilden Foundations)

derbilt's mother and friend of hers came for excitement. That went well until a white gentleman was found in the bathroom, I guess, dead. It wasn't clear whether he had been murdered or had just died, but that was the end of that place because Walter Winchell blew that incident up and that sort of put an end to Harlem's popularity as the nightclub mecca.

My brother and I went to Augusta Savage's Art School on 143rd Street, which was funded by the WPA. All the supplies were free, so my brother and I continued our artwork connected with the Augusta Savage School. And there we met these twins and struck up a friendship and later we were married. We got married on the same day and separated on the same night and we got our divorces at the same time. That was when we rented a loft on 141 West 125th Street, where the State Office Building is today. We were there for a year. At that time Norman Lewis, another artist of the community, had a studio there and he encouraged us to take space there. In the meantime, Mr. Frankel of the Apollo Theatre Group became aware of our doing photography and offered us space next door to the Apollo Theatre that had been occupied by an actor named Hamtry Harrington. . . . That's where we opened our second studio, on 125th Street at number 243. I say loft because we made the extra space into living quarters.

We had a very attractive place. We photographed a dance scene with Eartha Kitt and I went out and got evergreens to give it a tropical look. With Pearl Primus, I did the same thing. Maya Angelou was part of Pearl Primus's dance company and I photographed her, too. The studio was the place where everyone came. The street-level display attracted people to come up to the studio. I changed the display every three weeks at least. Many of the local photographers of the day never changed their displays. The display was of the girl of the week, the girl of the month. We used to do Miss Subway, which was a young black woman. It was like a meeting place. Of course, the girls came and then the fellas came—Belafonte, Poitier, Ruby Dee, Ray Robinson. We gave parties and Lady Day [Billie Holiday] and Count Basie and [boxer] Jack Johnson would all be there. We met them and we invited them and they came. We sent out a flyer and invited the celebrities of the day to the studio and we would take free photos and present them with the photos. Some of the people we photographed never stepped a foot into our studio, we had to go to them.

Mr. Smith discussed how he and his brother, Morgan, first became interested in photography:

We would carry the camera with us everywhere. It was a gift from a white person who had met us and was aware of our desire and made us a gift of the camera. There were no blacks taking pictures in our hometown. Of course, when we came to New York we brought the camera with us. And when we would go out—we liked to draw, we liked to sketch—we had sketch books that we carried. And riding on the subway, wherever we were, if people did not object, we would sketch. So the camera replaced the sketch pad, in some cases. And by having the camera, on Easter Sunday we would photograph various people in their dress and we submitted some of those photographs to the *Amsterdam News*.

Harlem started changing for me after WWII. Many of the people that I knew came back from the war as junkies. The restaurants and clubs opened up downtown to black people and many of the black businesses in Harlem started to decline.

The Smith Brothers documented Harlem life from the 1930s to the 1960s. They photographed black entertainers, politicians, sports personalities, and the everyday folks of the community. Their visual history of the famous black community, *Harlem—The Vision of Morgan and Marvin Smith* was published in 1998. Morgan Smith died in 1993 and Marvin Smith lives in New York City.

555 EDGECOMBE AVENUE (AT 160TH STREET)

This landmark building was home to singer-activist Paul Robeson, renowned bandleader Count Basie, and boxing champion Joe Louis.

MUSEUMS AND GALLERIES

THE STUDIO MUSEUM IN HARLEM

144 West 125th Street (Malcolm X and Adam Clayton
  Powell Jr. Boulevards)
(212) 864-4500; (212) 864-4800
www.studiomuseuminharlem.org

The Studio Museum exhibits contemporary and historical African American art, including paintings, prints, photographs, sculptures, and artifacts from America, Africa, the Caribbean, and Latin America. The museum's programs include the Artists-in-Residence Program, which provides gallery space to emerging artists, the Cooperative School Program, through which artists teach in Harlem schools, as well as workshops for individuals and families, talks, concerts, and demonstrations. The gift shop has a wonderful collection of books, calendars, postcards, and posters.

Open Wednesday through Sunday. Admission: $5; $3, students and seniors; $1, kids twelve and older, free for members and kids under twelve. Free for all the first Saturday of every month. Call for current exhibition information. (See sidebar, page 96.)

MORRIS-JUMEL MANSION AND MUSEUM

1765 Jumel Terrace (at 160th Street in Roger Morris Park)
(212) 923-8008

Built in 1765, the Greek Revival mansion is Manhattan's oldest existing residential building. Inside it has hand-painted Chinese wallpaper and mahogany Chippendale mirrors.

▼

THE STUDIO MUSEUM IN HARLEM

The Studio Museum in Harlem began in a loft in 1968 as a place for black artists excluded from gallery and museum shows to work and exhibit their art. The museum, located at 144 West 125th Street, has evolved into the leading presenter and interpreter of African American and African art in the United States. The Studio Museum was the first African American museum to be accredited (in 1987) by the American Association of Museums. Its permanent collection includes nineteenth-century African art, twentieth-century Caribbean and African art, and traditional African art and artifacts. Among the artists in the permanent collection are Romare Bearden, Jacob Lawrence, Betye Saar, and Philome Obin.

The Studio Museum presents four to five major exhibitions a year, including an exhibit featuring the work from the Artists-in-Residence program. Past exhibits include "The Decade Show: Frameworks of Identity" in the 1980s, "Memory and Metaphor: The Art of Romare Bearden, 1940–1987," and "Contemporary African Artists: Changing Tradition."

The museum's commitment to the community is evidenced in its extensive outreach and educational programs. The Artists-in-Residence Program offers three emerging artists of African descent fellowships, materials, and studio space for one year. An exhibit of the artists' work is shown every fall in the annual "From the Studio: Artists-in-Residence." The Cooperative School Program serves 24,000 students in the Harlem public schools through its in-school workshops and classes. The Intern Program provides museum training to African American college graduates. The Vital Expressions in American Art program is a series of lectures, concerts, films, symposia, poetry readings and performances that enhance and interpret the museum's exhibitions.

The museum's current 60,000-square-foot space houses two floors of galleries, studios, and workshop spaces, an outdoor sculpture garden, the museum store and cafe, an archive, and permanent storage spaces. The museum has begun a renovation and expansion project that will increase its space to 72,000 square feet, and will include permanent gallery space, an auditorium, and a new façade.

◆◆◆

The mansion was first the home of British Lieutenant Colonel Roger Morris and his wife, Mary Philipse Morris. During the American Revolution it was occupied by George Washington and later by British and Hessian militia. After the war it served as a tavern.

In 1810 Stephen Jumel, a French wine merchant and his wife, Eliza, bought the house. After Stephen passed away, Eliza married Aaron Burr, the former vice president of the United States, in 1833. Burr killed Alexander Hamilton (owner of Hamilton Grange, another country estate in Harlem) in a duel in 1804. (See page 95.)

Open Wednesday through Sunday, from 10:00 A.M. to 4:00 P.M. Group tours should call for reservations. Admission: $3; $2 students and seniors; free for kids under twelve.

Morris-Jumel Mansion at West 160th Street and Roger Morris Park (Photo by Linda Tarrant-Reid)

Jumel Terrace brownstones, between Sylvan Terrace and West 162nd Street (Photo by Linda Tarrant-Reid)

ESSIE GREEN GALLERIES
419A Convent Avenue (at West 148th Street)
(212) 368-9635

This intimate gallery is located in a restored brownstone in the famed Sugar Hill section of Harlem. It features the art of black masters Romare Bearden, William S. Carter, and Allen Stringfellow.

Open Tuesday through Saturday. Visits are by appointment only.

THE AFRICAN-AMERICAN WAX AND HISTORY MUSEUM OF HARLEM
316 West 115th Street (between Frederick Douglass
  Boulevard and Manhattan Avenue)
(212) 678-7818

Artist-sculptor Raven Chanticleer showcases his wax replicas of famous African American heroes, including Malcolm X, Mary

Wax figure of Dr. Martin Luther King Jr. at the African-American Black History and Wax Museum of Harlem (Photo by Raven Chanticleer)

McCleod Bethune, Martin Luther King Jr., Frederick Douglass, New York City's first black mayor, David Dinkins, and Duke Elllington. Founded in 1989, this small, quirky museum also has wood and wire sculptures and oil paintings of famous blacks, such as dancer-chanteuse Josephine Baker.

Open Tuesday through Sunday. Visits are by appointment only. Admission: $10; $5 kids under ten. Group rates available. Call for more information.

Schomburg Center for Research in Black Culture, at West 135th Street and Malcolm X Boulevard (Photo by Linda Tarrant-Reid)

Schomburg Center for Research in Black Culture
515 Malcolm X Boulevard (between West 135th and
   West 136th Streets)
(212) 491-2200

Devoted to the preservation of African American history and culture, this archive houses over five million items of black life, including art and artifacts, rare books and manuscripts, photographs and prints, motion pictures, and recorded sound. The New York Public Library's Division of Negro Literature, History, and Prints was originally located at the 135th Street branch in a three-story stone building. That building is now part of the Schomburg Center. In 1926 the collection of scholar and bibliophile Arthur A. Schomburg, which included 5,000 books, 3,000 manuscripts, 2,000 etchings and paintings, and several thousand pamphlets, was added to the New York Public Library's Division of Negro Literature. Schomburg was named curator of the division in 1932, and he remained there until his death in 1938. The collection was renamed in Schomburg's honor in 1940.

The Schomburg Center for Research in Black Culture opened at its present site in 1980. The Langston Hughes Auditorium opened in April of 1991. It mounts exhibitions of African American history and culture, as well as presents concerts, poetry readings, and plays. The Schomburg book store has a wide selection of books by and about people of color.

Open Monday through Saturday. Call for more information.

HARLEM EYES

The history of Harlem is documented in the photographs of many African American photographers. Four gentlemen began documenting the people, places, and events of this historic community starting in the early 1900s: James Van Der Zee, whose G.G.G. Studio was at 272 Lenox Avenue; Austin Hansen, who worked out of his basement studio at 232 West 135th Street; and the Smith Brothers, Marvin and Morgan, who worked out of a second-floor loft studio, next door to the famed Apollo Theatre, at 243 West 125th Street. The Schomburg Center for Research in Black Culture houses the photographic collections of these photographers. (See sidebar about Marvin Smith on pages 89–94.)

ADAM CLAYTON POWELL JR. GALLERY
State Office Building (at West 125th Street)
163 West 125th Street
(212) 749-5298/(212) 873-5040

Located on the second floor of the State Office Building, the gallery is a revolving exhibition space that features the works of African American painters, sculptors, and photographers in six to eight exhibits a year. The gallery also sponsors a film series. Call for more information.

CULTURAL CENTERS

AARON DAVIS HALL
City College of New York
West 135th Street (at Convent Avenue)
(212) 650-7148

This three-theater complex is a major venue for performances by culturally diverse artists including musicians, composers, poets, dancers, choreographers, filmmakers, and writers. As Harlem's principal center for the performing arts, Aaron Davis Hall presents nationally and internationally recognized talent as well as emerging artists.

The box office is open Tuesday through Saturday. Call for a performance schedule.

THE FRANK SILVERA WRITERS' WORKSHOP
(212) 281-8832
www.artswire.org/~playrite

The mission of this writers workshop is to recognize and cultivate the talent of aspiring and emerging black playwrights, directors, actors, producers, and designers. The workshop offers a reading and critique series, a weekly seminar series, and a playwriting series. Call for more information or check Web site for workshop and performance schedule.

THE FREDERICK DOUGLASS CREATIVE ARTS CENTER
270 West 96th Street (between Broadway
  and West End Avenue)
(212) 864-3375
www.fdcac.org

This creative arts center has launched the careers of many success-ful writers. Founded in 1971 by executive director Fred Hudson and Budd Schulberg, the center's writers development program offers screenwriting, playwriting, television writing, poetry, and feature-article writing workshops. There are also workshops in acting, radio, and video production. The center hosts the annual Black Roots Fes-tival of poetry, prose, drama, and music every spring. Past partici-pants in the festival include writers Toni Morrison, Maya Angelou, Gwendolyn Brooks, Terry McMillan, Quincy Troupe, and others.

ROGER FURMAN THEATRE
253 West 138th Street
(212) 926-0104

Begun in 1964, the Roger Furman Theatre is one of the oldest theater companies in Harlem. It provides a showcase for quality black and Hispanic playwrights, directors, performing artists, tech-nicians, and designers. Performances are held at the Schomburg Center for Research in Black Culture and Aaron Davis Hall (see pages 100–101 and 102). Call for a performance schedule.

H.A.D.L.E.Y. PLAYERS
207 West 133rd Street
(212) 862-1179

The Harlem Artist Development League Especially for You (H.A.D.L.E.Y.) was started in 1979 by Gertrude Jeannette. The league presents three major plays annually, as well as poetry readings, play readings, and acting classes for beginning and advanced students. Performances take place in the basement of

the historic St. Philips Church at 204 West 134th Street. Call for
more information.

THE NATIONAL BLACK THEATRE
2031 Fifth Avenue (at 125th Street)
(212) 360-7609; (212) 722-3800

Executive director Barbara Ann Teer has been a creative force in
the Harlem community for over thirty years. She continues to
provide a view into the African and West Indian traditions of
the performing arts through the National Black Theatre. This
community-based company is the recipient of numerous awards
for its work. Offerings include theatrical performances, workshops,
children's programs, events, and tours. Call for more information.

THE BOYS CHOIR AND GIRLS CHOIR OF HARLEM
2005 Madison Avenue (127th Street)
(212) 289-6227

The choirs are composed of predominantly African American and
Hispanic youth who perform every kind of music from classical to
jazz, including contemporary songs and gospel. Their annual schedule includes two national tours and one international tour. The
Boys Choir, which was formed in 1968, has performed with leading
artists and orchestras, appeared on Broadway, toured the world,
and recorded several soundtracks for feature films. The Girls Choir
was established in 1979. Call for a performance schedule.

THE DANCE THEATRE OF HARLEM
466 West 152nd Street (between St. Nicholas and
   Amsterdam Avenues)
(212) 690-2800

This predominantly black ballet company was founded by Arthur
Mitchell, a former principal dancer and the first full-time black

The Boys Choir of Harlem (Photo courtesy of The Boys Choir of Harlem)

member of the New York City Ballet, and Karel Shook in 1969. It performs a diverse neoclassical repertoire that includes over 112 works by choreographers Geoffrey Holder, George Balanchine, and others. The company has toured the United States and abroad, with long-term residencies in Detroit and at the Kennedy Center for Performing Arts in Washington, D.C. The Dance Theatre's company school offers classes to kids, teens, and adults. Dance Theatre hosts an open-house performance once a month. Call for more information.

THE HARLEM SCHOOL OF THE ARTS
645 St. Nicholas Avenue (between West 141st
   and West 145th Streets)
(212) 926-4100

Since 1964 this special school has offered classes to students from pre-kindergarten to adult in dance, drama, music, and the visual arts. Its founder, soprano Dorothy Maynor, believed that an arts education stimulates children emotionally and intellectually and strengthens the family bond through its commitment to the child's development.

Call for more information.

Dance Theater of Harlem soloist Ramon Thielen in *Manifestations* (Photo by Frank Capri)

OTHER PLACES OF INTEREST

RIVERBANK STATE PARK
Entrance at 145th Street and Riverside Drive (between
    138th and 145th Streets)

Overlooking the Hudson River, this twenty-eight-acre park has an indoor Olympic-size pool, an outdoor pool and wading pond, football and softball fields, basketball, handball, and tennis courts, a cultural center, and a rink for ice- or roller-skating. There are also picnic grounds and play areas for kids.

JACKIE ROBINSON PARK
145th to 155th Streets (between Edgecombe and Bradhurst Avenues)

Named for baseball legend Jackie Robinson, this lush park has a swimming pool, basketball and volleyball courts, bandshell, baseball field, and playground. In 1947 Robinson broke the color barrier when he joined the Brooklyn Dodgers, becoming the first African American to play major-league baseball. In 1949 Jackie Robinson was named the National Baseball League's Most Valuable Player.

GENERAL GRANT NATIONAL MEMORIAL
Riverside Drive at 122nd Street
(212) 666-1640

The granite dome structure known as Grant's Tomb was completed in 1897 and is the final resting place of General Ulysses S. Grant (1822–1885), the eighteenth president of the United States (1869–1877), and his wife, Julie. Grant was commander-in-chief of the Union Army during the Civil War. His contributions are depicted in an exhibit within the tomb that spans his early years, the Civil War years, and the end of his life. Situated on a hill overlooking the Hudson River, the park surrounding Grant's Tomb is the site of the summer Jazzmobile Concerts.

Open Monday through Sunday. Free admission.

THE RIVERSIDE CHURCH
490 Riverside Dr. (at 120th Street)
(212) 870-6700
www.theriversidechurchny.org

This church is interdenominational, interracial, and international with a congregation of more than 2,400 members and affiliates.

Constructed in 1927, Riverside Church is modeled after a thirteenth-century Gothic cathedral in Chartres, France. Its 20-floor tower contains meeting rooms and the 74-bell Laura Spelman Rockefeller Memorial Carillon, which has the largest tuned bell in the world. Members and visitors can participate in a number of outreach programs that benefit the community, including the health and wellness ministry, youth programs, bible study and prayer groups, seminars, lectures, task forces on AIDS, education, and peace and disarmament, a prison ministry, and a South Africa Initiative. Many noted social and political activists have spoken at the church, including the Reverend Dr. Martin Luther King Jr., former president of South Africa Nelson Mandela, and Children's Defense Fund Head Marian Wright-Edelman.

DINING OUT

Food is an integral part of the African American experience in New York City. The aromas wafting through many African American, African, and Caribbean homes on any given Sunday afternoon or holiday are duplicated at the many eateries listed in this section. Visitors can sample a variety of offerings throughout New York City. From traditional soul food, to West African, to Caribbean cuisine, foodies can taste delectably diverse dishes in restaurants ranging from tiny takeout joints, to elegantly appointed boîtes, to quaint cafes. Enjoy these tasty dishes in warm and welcoming atmospheres in a range of prices.

MISS MAMIE'S SPOONBREAD TOO
366 West 110th Street (between Columbus and
   Manhattan Avenues)
(212) 865-6744

This tiny dining room serving mouthwatering Southern cuisine is down the street from the Cathedral of St. John the Divine. The homey, brightly decorated restaurant offers a menu that promises the diner "it's like going back home!" Soul food standards of Southern fried chicken, Mamie Jean's Smothered Chicken, and North Carolina BBQ Ribs are partnered with a choice of two sides: Macaroni and Cheese, Candied Yams, Collard Greens, String Beans, Mashed Potatoes, or Peas and Rice. The delicious homemade dessert offerings include Fruit Cobbler of the Day, Miss Mamie's Banana Pudding, Sweet Potato Pie, and a Cake of the Day. The multilayered Coconut Cake is to die for.

Open seven days a week from Noon to 10:00 P.M. Major credit cards accepted. Delivery available for orders $15 and over.

MISS MAUDE'S SPOONBREAD TOO
547 Malcom X Boulevard (between West 137th
  and West 138th Streets)
(212) 690-3100

This is the sister restaurant to Miss Mamie's, serving an identical menu of finger lickin' soul food.

Open seven days a week for lunch and dinner. Major credit cards accepted.

EMILY'S
1325 Fifth Avenue (at East 111th Street)
(212) 996-1212

This is an intimate, cozy oasis on Harlem's east side, near the statue of jazz legend Duke Ellington. The kitchen provides an array of soul food offerings, including the old standbys—Smothered Pork Chops, Fried Chicken, Potato Salad, Collard Greens, and Macaroni and Cheese.

Open seven days a week for lunch and dinner. Brunch served on Saturday and Sunday. Major credit cards accepted.

There is a significant African community in Harlem. Many of these residents migrated from West Africa and have settled around 116th Street. The blocks between Malcolm X and Frederick Douglass Boulevards are dotted with African restaurants, stores, and fabric shops. One restaurant that is located near the Malcolm Shabazz Marketplace on 116th Street and Fifth Avenue, an easy walk from the market is listed below.

AFRICA
247 West 116th Street (between Adam Clayton Powell Jr.
  and Frederick Douglass Boulevards)
(212) 666-9400

This popular Senegalese restaurant has ornately carved chairs that belie its informality. The diner can choose between delicacies such as *Thiébu Djen*—an exotic stew of whitefish, eggplant, carrots, cassava, and cabbage in a spicy tomato sauce over rice—or Chicken *Yassa,* a marinated lemon chicken with sautéed onions served over rice. Marinated Lamb with Vegetables, in a creamy, rich peanut butter sauce, is also a tantalizing choice. Beverages include *Bissap* Juice, a sorrel-like fruit drink, and a homemade ginger drink.
    Open seven days a week for lunch and dinner.

Two excellent Ethiopian restaurants and a Senegalese restaurant, below, are located near Columbia University on Amsterdam Avenue and Broadway.

MASSAWA
1239 Amsterdam Avenue (121st Street)
(212) 663-0505

Traditional Ethiopian and Eritrean dishes are on the menu at this restaurant located in the Columbia University neighborhood. The menu invites the diner to eat with their hands, as is done in Ethiopia. Some of the dishes, such as *Kitfo* (lean beef seasoned with clarified butter, cardamom, and cayenne) and *Tebsie Derho* (boneless chicken breasts, green peppers, and garlic) can be ordered either spicy or mild. For the not-so-adventurous, there is

Spaghetti with Meat Sauce, and Tuna Salad. There is also a selection of vegetarian dishes on the menu. Massawa offers a reasonably priced lunch buffet Monday through Friday.

Open seven days a week for lunch and dinner. Free delivery with a minimum of two orders. Major credit cards accepted.

Zula Cafe and Restaurant
1260 Amsterdam Avenue (122nd Street)
(212) 663-1670

This Ethiopian restaurant is down the street from Massawa and offers many of the same dishes, which means diners should ask the server if a dish is spicy or not. *Kitfo* is described on this menu as lean, chopped raw beef seasoned with spiced butter and served with *mitmita* (hot sauce) and yogurt. *Zegenie* is a seasoned beef stew with spicy sauce and a specialty butter. The extensive vegetarian menu offers combination plates of chick peas, vegetables, and lentils.

Open seven days a week for lunch and dinner. Major credit cards accepted.

Obaa Koryoe
3143 Broadway (between Tiemann Place and LaSalle
   Street, near 125th Street)
(212) 316-2950

Specializing in West African Cuisine, the restaurant offers a varied menu for lunch and dinner, including some vegetarian dishes. Entrees of Cow Foot, Lamb, or Goat Stew are cooked with fresh ground spices in a tomato sauce and are served with a choice of *Jolloff* (tomatoes and rice), *Wachey* (black-eyed peas and rice), or white rice. Authentic African dishes include Fried or Baked Fish served with freshly ground hot pepper, onions, tomatoes, and *kenkey* (sour cornmeal), *Banku* served with okra and the soup of the day, or *Baa-Flor* (cornmeal) with a choice of chicken, fish, lamb, tripe, or beef. Boiled green or yellow plantains are served with sunflower seed sauce and a choice of beef, chicken, oxtail, tripe, or fish. Vegetarians can enjoy Bean Stew with Fried Yellow

Plantains, Broccoli with Home-Styled Sauce (served with *Wachey* or *Jolloff* rice), or the Gary Byrd Special: a spaghetti dish with mixed vegetables and mushroom sauce.

Open seven days a week. Free delivery on orders $12 and over. Major credit cards accepted.

STRICTLY ROOTS
2058 Adam Clayton Powell Boulevard (at 123rd Street)
(212) 864-8699

The sign at this Harlem take-out vegetarian restaurant boasts: "We serve nothing that crawls, walks, swims or flies." Offerings include Vegetable Lasagna, Tofu Stew, Sweet-and-Sour Tofu, and an array of soy and wheat dishes.

Open Monday through Saturday. Major credit cards accepted.

PERK'S FINE CUISINE
553 Manhattan Avenue (123rd Street)
(212) 666-8500

This elegant uptown nightspot is a favorite of sports figures and celebrities. Dinner offerings include Golden Crab Cakes, made of fresh lump crabmeat, Lobster Bisque, Cajun Red Snapper, and Short Ribs of Beef, which are braised in their own juices. Live music is available Monday through Saturday.

Open for dinner Monday through Saturday. Mastercard and Visa accepted. (See page 127.)

RENCHER'S CRAB INN
15 West 125th Street (Fifth Avenue and Malcolm X
   Boulevard)
(212) 876-6664
www.crabinn.com

Treat yourself to Maryland-style crabs in the Cajun tradition at this attractive seafood restaurant right on the main drag of 125th

Street. Also on the menu are Dungeness Crabs, Alaskan King Crab Legs, and Snow Crabs. Other entrees include Shrimp Scampi, Soft-Shell Crabs, Clams on the Half Shell, Lobster, and Scallops. All served with sides of Baked Potato or French Fries and Corn on the Cob or Coleslaw.

Open for lunch and dinner seven days a week. Major credit cards accepted.

UPTOWN JUICE BAR
54 West 125th Street (between Fifth Avenue and
   Malcolm X Boulevard)
(212) 987-2660

Tucked away between retail stores on the thriving 125th Street commercial strip, the bright green awning beckons you to this little oasis. Take the juice cure to fix what ails you. Whether you have a hangover, stress, P.M.S., depression, or hair loss, the Uptown Juice Bar says it has an elixir to soothe your complaint. This neighborhood haunt also offers an extensive menu of vegetarian delights, including Ital Stew, Barbecue Soy Chunks, Vegetarian Pizza and Lasagna, Couscous, Veggie Burgers, and lots more.

Open seven days a week.

M & G DINER
383 West 125th Street (at Morningside Avenue)
(212) 864-7326

Open 24 hours a day, seven days a week, this southern-style diner's breakfast menu includes Beef or Pork Patty Sausages with Home Fries and Eggs, or Salmon Croquettes with Grits and Eggs Served with Biscuits or Toast. The dinner menu features delectable Short Ribs of Beef, Barbecue Ribs, Fried Chicken, Meatloaf, or scrumptious Chicken and Dumplings. M & G also serves up Fried Pork Chops, Ham Hocks, and Chitterlings. Its jukebox is filled with the best selection of blues and R&B tunes that only enhance this stick-to-the ribs, down-home fare.

THE COTTON CLUB
656 West 125th Street (near the West Side Highway)
(212) 663-7980

Named for the original Cotton Club of the Harlem Renaissance, which was located at 644 Lenox Avenue (Malcolm X Boulevard), this newer version offers sustenance for body and spirit. The lip-smacking buffet of Fried Chicken, Black-Eyed Peas and Rice, Mixed Vegetables, Candied Yams, and Macaroni and Cheese is a sight to behold. On Sundays experience their famous gospel brunch featuring tantalizing Southern cuisine and the soul-searing music of a gospel group. The Sunday gospel brunch is a definite "must do" for a hand-clapping, foot-stomping good time.

Open Thursday through Monday for dinner. Jazz on Thursday, Friday, and Saturday. Sunday gospel brunch. Reservations recommended. Visa and MasterCard accepted. (See page 126, and sidebar on pages 130–131).

BAYOU
308 Malcolm X Boulevard—Second Floor (between West
   125th and West 126th Street)
(212) 426-3800

The latest star in Harlem's culinary constellation is a New Orleans-inspired boîte whose menu is chock-full of "Big Easy" delights such as Crawfish Étouffée, Shrimp and Okra Gumbo, and Turtle Soup. Former president Bill Clinton gave the intimate eatery his seal of approval on a recent visit when he sampled the Gumbo and the Red Beans and Rice.

Open for lunch Monday through Friday, dinner Monday through Saturday, and brunch on Sunday. Major credit cards accepted.

Jimmy's Uptown

2207 Adam Clayton Powell Jr. Boulevard (between
   West 130th and West 131st Streets)
(212) 491-4000

The owner of Jimmy's Bronx Cafe saw an opportunity and jumped on it with the opening of Jimmy's Uptown. The sleek, modern open-floor plan, punctuated by wood, leather, and diaphanous drapes, transports diners to another place and time. The ultra-hip clientele dines on the palate-pleasing Latin-soul cuisine while people-watching. Tamarind Roast Salmon with Mustard Greens and Orange Relish, Cabernet-Braised Short Ribs accompanied by Malanga Mash and Roasted Baby Vegetables, as well as the Seafood Paella are deliciously rendered by this innovative kitchen. For seafood lovers, the raw bar is stocked daily with fresh offerings from the sea.

Open for dinner Monday through Sunday. Major credit cards accepted. Reservations recommended.

Sylvia's

328 Malcolm X Boulevard (between West 126th
   and West 127th Streets)
(212) 996-0660

Sylvia Woods, Harlem's own "Queen of Soul Food," offers a menu of delectable dishes at this world famous restaurant. Busloads of visitors from all over the world come to sample the Fried Chicken, Baked Ham, Fried Whiting, Candied Yams, Collard Greens, Potato Salad, Barbecue Ribs, and Sweet Corn Bread. Breakfast includes such tasty morsels as Sautéed Chicken Livers and Grits, Salmon Cakes and Eggs, as well as Fried Pork Chop, Fried Chicken, or Sausage and Eggs. Sylvia's also has a line of retail food products for sale at the restaurant and at select food stores across the United States.

Open seven days a week for breakfast, lunch, and dinner. Major credit cards and debit cards accepted. (See photo and sidebar on page 116.)

▼

SYLVIA'S RESTAURANT
QUEEN OF SOUL FOOD

Sylvia's Restaurant, 328 Malcolm X Boulevard between West 126th and West 127th Streets (Photo by Linda Tarrant-Reid)

The sprawling 350-seat soul food restaurant at 328 Malcolm X Boulevard and 126th Street is legendary. Tour buses line up in front of the famous restaurant on any given day and discharge hungry passengers from places as far away as Japan, France, and Germany, and as nearby as Philadelphia, Baltimore, and Washington, D.C. Folks from Southern California and Massachusetts also beat a path to the door to partake of what has become known as the best soul food this side of the Rockies.

Sylvia and her husband Herbert Woods opened their restaurant in 1962 at 338 Lenox Avenue (now Malcolm X Boulevard). Sylvia worked in the original eatery as a waitress, and when the owners decided to sell, she and Herbert bought the place. They moved to their current location at number 328, a few doors down the street, in 1968. Raised in the South by her widowed mother, Sylvia and her late sister Louise learned to cook and take care of themselves at an early age. They worked hard to make ends meet. They planted crops and sold tobacco before coming to New York City, where Louise opened a restaurant at 121st Street and Lenox Avenue (now Malcolm X Boulevard). The restaurant, named Louise's Restaurant, is still operating.

Sylvia Woods's reputation as the "Queen of Soul Food" was earned through years of hard work by her and her entire family. The Woods's children and grandchildren grew up in the business that serves delicious soul food including favorites like macaroni and cheese, collard greens, potato salad, barbecue ribs, and smothered chicken.

The walls of the restaurant are lined with photographs of famous diners, including actors Lou Gossette Jr. and Richard Gere, singers Janet Jackson and Roberta Flack, Reverend Jesse Jackson, and former Secretary of State Madeline Albright.

This successful family business has expanded and includes a retail food line of Sylvia's own recipes of tasty vegetables, sauces, seasonings, and cookies. The products are available in New York at local ShopRite and Pathmark supermarkets and in stores in California and throughout the southern United States.

FLORIDITA
3219 Broadway (126th Street)
(212) 662-0266

This popular Cuban restaurant, nestled under the elevated trains near the West Side Highway, is famous for its Café con Lêche, half milk and half Colombian coffee, as well as its *Pollo Asado* (broiled chicken with rice and beans and fried plantains), and the *Mofongo con Chicharrones* (fried mashed plantains with pork crackling). American dishes, including Beef Stew, Fried Pork Chops, Steak, and Lobster, are also available.

Open seven days a week for lunch and dinner. Floridita has another location at 3451 Broadway between 140th and 141st Streets [phone (212) 926-0319]. Major credit cards accepted.

GARY'S JAMAICAN HOT POT
2260 Adam Clayton Powell Jr. Boulevard (133rd Street)
(212) 491-5270

This small but popular dining spot offers the tastes of the Caribbean, including Curried Chicken, Curried Goat, Hot and Spicy Jerk Chicken, Oxtails, Short Ribs of Beef, and Escovietch (a choice of pan-fried whiting, snapper, or king fish simmered in herbs and spices). Sides include Rice and Peas, Collard Greens, Cabbage, Fried Plantains, Candied Yams, and Callaloo (when in season).

Open seven days a week. Major credit cards accepted.

WELLS SUPPER CLUB SITE
2247 Adam Clayton Powell Jr. Boulevard (132nd Street)

Although closed for renovations since 1999, this black institution was the home of the famous Chicken and Waffles combo. This historic restaurant which opened in 1938, offered a New Orleans–style and traditional soul cuisine. (See sidebar on page 119.)

22 WEST RESTAURANT AND LOUNGE
22 West 135th Street (between Fifth Avenue
   and Malcolm X Boulevard)
(212) 862-7770

This informal neighborhood restaurant across from Harlem Hospital was a favorite haunt of civil rights activist Malcolm X. Serving breakfast, lunch, and traditional soul food dinners of Liver and Onions, Oxtails, Smothered Chicken, Chitterlings, and Barbecued Ribs, it's a great place to get a good meal.

Open seven days a week. Major credit cards accepted.

ELIZABETH WELLS, OWNER OF WELLS SUPPER CLUB

Elizabeth Wells, owner of Wells Supper Club
(Photo by Linda Tarrant-Reid)

Elizabeth Wells was interviewed by the author in 1999, before the famous Wells Supper Club closed for renovations. Although the restaurant has not reopened, Mrs. Wells's story is an integral part of Harlem's history.

My late husband, Joseph P. Wells, opened the restaurant in May of 1938 at 2247 Seventh Avenue, which is our current location. It was and still is a family-owned and operated business. After my husband passed away, I took over the business, and during that time I have seen the neighborhood change. I see many different people in the community—a mixture of different cultures, ethnic backgrounds, and races.

In 1963, when I first came to Harlem, the community was in the midst of a transition. I saw lots of things happening— race riots, the State Office Building was [being built], and vendors and booksellers who used to sell their wares at sidewalk stands disappearing. The community has been through quite a lot, and our businesses reflect that. Our restaurant has been through changes as well. There is a lot of competition. McDonald's came, then Burger King, and many more restaurants have followed.

Joseph Wells is credited with creating the now-famous Harlem combo of fried chicken and waffles. It is a dish that is replicated over and over at soul food restaurants everywhere. Mrs. Wells recounted how the dish came about.

In the earlier years, when my husband Joseph first started the restaurant, most of the restaurants in the community were selling hash and eggs. My husband wanted to sell something different, so he thought he would try chicken and waffles because it would serve two purposes. It could be a breakfast meal and a dinner meal, and it could be served anytime. Nobody would touch it, they did not want to eat their fried chicken with syrup and waffles. So he said, "I better start giving it away." And as he gave it away the word of mouth spread, and after a while it was able to sustain itself and took off. Well, it became a Harlem delicacy, I would say. Now everybody is trying to serve it.

My husband was from Fort Gaines, Georgia. And I am from New Orleans, Louisiana. So the menu reflects both of our roots and consists of mostly Southern foods along with the famous Chicken and Waffles. We serve a very eclectic clientele. When the restaurant first started, we served customers from the surrounding community as well as many famous people. Paul Robeson was a regular customer. Harry Belafonte and Sidney Poitier would also eat at Wells. Nat King Cole and his wife had their wedding reception here. They were married at Abyssinian

Baptist Church on West 138th Street. My husband and Nat King Cole's sister-in-law Charlotte were good friends, and she arranged for the reception to be here.

Many celebrities still come to eat at Wells. They sit quietly, and our customers and staff respect their privacy. Hip-hop music star Foxy Brown and her entourage have eaten at Wells. Dancer and choreographer Geoffrey Holder and politicians like Congressman Charles Rangel have enjoyed meals here.

Count Basie's Club used to be located right next door. I remember one night we had Frank Sinatra, Dean Martin, and Sammy Davis Jr. come over to eat after being at Count Basie's. They were called the Rat Pack back then. Now we get a lot of European and Japanese tourists for Sunday brunch. We have music during the week and on weekends, so that brings in a lot people. We're continuing the tradition that my late husband began.

Cafe Largo

3387 Broadway (between West 137th and West 138th Streets)
(212) 862-8142

Cafe Largo serves Spanish cuisine, including yellow or white rice and black or red beans, and baked, grilled, or fried chicken—the menu also offers lasagna. San Cho, a heavy, rich soup of chicken, rice, and tomatoes, is a meal in itself.

Open seven days a week. Major credit cards accepted.

Pan Pan

500 Malcolm X Boulevard (West 135th Street)
(212) 926-4900

This no-frills dining institution is located across from the Schomburg Center for Research in Black Culture and Harlem Hospital.

The Chicken and Waffles are to die for—the waffles' crunchy exterior and spongy interior are perfectly paired with the best fried chicken this side of 135th Street. Other dishes include the Chopped Barbecue Sandwich, Oxtail Stew, and a host of standard Southern delicacies.

Open seven days a week for breakfast, lunch, and dinner.

Sugar Shack Cafe
2611 Frederick Douglass Boulevard (between West 139th
   and West 140th Streets)
(212) 491-4422

Located near Strivers' Row, this local favorite offers Southern cuisine with a twist. Start with the popular Whiting Fingers or the jumbo, golden Fried Shrimp, or the Soup du Jour. Entrees include the ubiquitous Chicken and Waffles, Vegetable Lasagna, Shrimp Scampi, and Smothered Soulful Chicken, which can be paired with Red Beans and Rice, Macaroni and Cheese, Collard Greens, or Candied Yams. For dessert, devour the heavenly Coconut Layer Cake with Pineapple Filling, or sample the ultimate New York Cheese Cake or the Old-Fashioned Apple Pie.

Open Tuesday through Sunday. Major credit cards accepted. (See page 125.)

Londel's Supper Club
2620 Frederick Douglass Boulevard (between West 139th
   and West 140th Streets)
(212) 234-6114

Cajun, continental, and Southern traditional fare is what's served in this elegant Harlem establishment. The well-seasoned Blackened Catfish with Collard Greens, Seasoned Rice, and the Sauteed Spinach are all to die for. For seafood lovers the Sauteed Whiting with White Wine and Butter Sauce is a must-eat. Grilled Chicken Breast with Dijon Mustard Cream Sauce and Farm-Fresh Sauteed

String Beans, plus the Macaroni and Cheese and Candied Yams are winners on this extensive menu. For dessert try Londel's Own Bread Pudding with Rum Sauce, the Sweet Potato Pie with a dollop of whipped cream, or sample the Cheesecake with Strawberry Sauce.

Open Tuesday through Saturday for lunch and dinner. Brunch served Sunday. Major credit cards accepted. (See page 125.)

FAMOUS FISH MARKET
684 St. Nicholas Avenue (West 145th Street)
(212) 491-8323

Only three people at a time can fit into this popular Harlem landmark, which serves Fried Fish, Shrimp, Clams, Oysters, Scallops, and Salmon Steaks—with French Fries or without—to hungry regulars. Coleslaw is also on the menu as a side, but it's merely a diversion to those folks who want the real deal. By lunchtime and into late afternoon, the line snakes out the door of this tiny, basement take-out joint as patrons wait to place their orders.

Open seven days a week for lunch and dinner.

CHARLES' SOUTHERN STYLE KITCHEN
2841 Frederick Douglass Boulevard (between West 151st
    and West 152nd Streets)
(212) 926-4313

For a reasonable price, diners get a wonderful selection of soul food dishes and a great deal. Southern standards like Fried, Baked, or Smothered Chicken are served with sides of Mixed Vegetables, Collard Greens, Cabbage, Yams, Okra and Tomatoes, Macaroni and Cheese, or Black-Eyed Peas. For fish lovers, there's also Salmon Cakes, Baked Blue Fish, or Fried Whiting. Pig's Feet, Barbecued Pork Ribs, and Oxtails are also on the menu.

Open seven days a week for lunch and dinner. Eat in or take out.

COPELAND'S RESTAURANT
547 West 145th Street (between Broadway
  and Amsterdam Avenue)
(212) 234-2356

This Hamilton Heights restaurant serves up tantalizing soul food dishes, including Fried Chicken, Short Ribs of Beef, and Smothered Pork Chops, paired with sides of Macaroni and Cheese, Collard Greens, or Okra and Tomatoes. Folks come from near and far to sample the delicious dishes. For dessert, feast on Homemade Banana Pudding, Peach Cobbler, Bread Pudding with Grand Marnier Sauce, and Sweet Potato Pie.

Open Tuesday thorugh Sunday for dinner. Brunch served Sunday. Major credit cards accepted.

COPELAND'S CAFETERIA
549 West 145th Street (between Broadway
  and Amsterdam Avenue)
(212) 234-2356

Right next door to Copeland's, this cafeteria-style eatery is also called Reliables and is open Monday through Sunday for breakfast, lunch, and dinner. The restaurant offers an abbreviated soul food menu with similar dishes as the parent restaurant in a less formal setting. Takeout is available. Major credit cards accepted.

LIVE MUSIC

ST. NICK'S PUB
773 St. Nicholas Avenue (West 149th Street)
(212) 283-9728

Monday nights rock at this legendary joint's weekly jam session. Don't be surprised by who you might hear at this historic club. Stevie Wonder, Broadway singer-actress Lilias White, and jazz vocalist Cassandra Wilson have all held the audience spellbound at one time or another.

Open mic on Wednesday. Live jazz every night except Tuesday. Showtime is at 9:00 P.M. Cover charge is $3, with a two-drink minimum. Call for more information.

LONDEL'S SUPPER CLUB
2620 Frederick Douglass Boulevard (between West 139th
  and West 140th Streets)
(212) 234-6114

This elegant Harlem etablishment serves up live jazz on the weekends. Showtimes are at 8:00 P.M. and 10:00 P.M. Cover charge is $5 with a two-drink minimum. Call for more information. (See page 122).

SUGAR SHACK CAFE
2611 Frederick Douglass Boulevard (between West 139th
  and West 140th Streets)
(212) 491-4422

This attractive spot has weekly entertainment featuring open-mic poetry on Wednesday nights and live jazz every Saturday. Call for more information. (See page 122.)

SYLVIA'S
328 Malcolm X Boulevard (between West 126th and
  West 127th Streets)
(212) 996-0660

On Saturdays, Sylvia's hosts a jazz and blues brunch with the Lonnie Youngblood Trio. The gospel brunch on Sundays with husband-and-wife singers Clay and Ruth Simpson will have you clapping your hands and tapping your feet. Major credit cards accepted. Call for more information.

The Cotton Club restaurant, at 656 West 125th
Street, was named for the famous nightclub that
closed in 1940. (Photo by Linda Tarrant-Reid)

COTTON CLUB
656 West 125th Street
(212) 663-7980

Enjoy the all-you-can eat soul food buffet and listen to the strains
of swing on Monday and jazz on Thursday, Friday, and Saturday.
Gospel brunch is served on Sundays. Major credit cards accepted.
Call for more information. (See pages 114 and 129, and sidebar on
page 130).

THE LENOX LOUNGE
288 Malcolm X Boulevard (between 124th
   and 125th Streets)
(212) 427-0253

This landmark club has been a fixture in Harlem since 1942. The
joint jumps with live jazz Thursday through Monday. There is no

cover on Thursdays, but the cover charge varies from Friday through Sunday. Major credit cards accepted. Call for more information.

SHOWMANS
375 West 125th Street (at St. Nicholas Avenue)
(212) 864-8941

This famous 1940s nightspot is a magnet for the who's who in show business and other famous and not-so-famous denizens of the Harlem community. Live jazz is offered Monday through Thursday at 8:30 P.M.; Friday and Saturday is at 10:30 P.M. There is no cover charge but there is a two-drink minimum per person, per show. Major credit cards accepted. Call for more information.

PERK'S FINE CUISINE
553 Manhattan Avenue (West 123rd Street)
(212) 666-8500

This attractive restaurant-club features Blues Mondays and Jazz Tuesdays. On Wednesday and Thursday vocalists and instrumentalists perform live in the multi-level jazz cocktail lounge. A DJ pumps up the volume on Friday and Saturday. Major credit cards accepted. Call for more information. (See page 112.)

JUMPIN' JOINTS

During the Jazz Age from the 1920s to 1940s, Harlem was the place to party. The Prohibition Act of 1920 (which was repealed in 1933) forbade the sale of liquor, and that inspired members of the underworld to seek out places where they could sell their illegal booze. Harlem attracted gangsters, slumming socialites, and the best music this side of the Mississippi. The black enclave was in full bloom with the success of the 1921 Broadway smash *Shuffle Along* and the birth of the "Cakewalk" dance craze. Thus began the trek to Harlem's many nightspots. As the mystique of Harlem grew, white people became increasingly curious.

Although many of the Renaissance clubs no longer exist, the addresses of these hot spots are part of the rich history of Harlem.

ALAMO CAFE
253 West 125th Street (1915–1925)

This rowdy club was located in the basement of what is now the world famous Apollo Theatre. When the club first opened, the house pianist was none other than Jimmy Durante. It became the Swanee, a black club, in 1925.

ALHAMBRA BALLROOM
2110 Seventh Avenue (1929–1945)

One of the famous jazz clubs where the top bands played.

BABY GRAND CAFE
319 West 125th Street (1945–1965)

The black and white façade was done up like a baby grand piano, keys and all. This was a regular stop of comedian Nipsey Russell, a frequent performer at the Apollo Theatre down the street at number 253.

COUNT BASIE'S LOUNGE
2245 Seventh Avenue (1955–1964)

Located right next door to Wells Supper Club, this bar was owned by bandleader Count Basie and had live music nightly.

BASEMENT BROWNIES
152 West 133rd Street (1930–1935)

This club was the first speakeasy in Harlem, which means you had to know someone to get in. Fats Waller and Art Tatum played here. After prohibition ended the club became an after-hours spot.

CONNIE'S INN
2221 Seventh Avenue (1921–1940)

A popular basement cabaret that was originally named the Shuffle Inn after the hit Broadway musical *Shuffle Along*. The large club had a nightly revue with dancers, singers, and musicians. Fats Waller's *Hot Chocolate* revue was performed at Connie's and produced such hits as "Ain't Misbehavin'," "That Rhythm Man," and "Savannah Sue." The club attracted white party-goers from downtown. After hours, this joint sizzled with jam sessions by the top musicians of the time that lasted until the wee hours of the morning.

COTTON CLUB
644 Lenox Avenue (1923–1936)

Bought by the crime syndicate headed by Owney Madden in 1922, the club opened after an elaborate renovation in 1923 as the Cotton Club. The jungle theme, the beautiful café au lait chorines, and the bootlegged booze were a huge draw for white patrons looking for an evening of exotic fun uptown. Duke Ellington's Cotton Club Band provided the music for the "whites only" audience. The club closed in 1940. (See sidebar on page 130.)

HARLEM OPERA HOUSE
209 West 125th Street (1889–1959)

This was a legitimate opera house built by Oscar Hammerstein I that eventually became part of a chain of vaudeville theaters. When blacks moved into Harlem the theater became a venue for black vaudeville acts and swing bands. The opera house also hosted Wednesday amateur nights, where wannabe entertainers would sing and tell jokes. When the Apollo opened in 1934, they also instituted a Wednesday amateur night which became very successful. With the Apollo's increased popularity, audiences stopped patronizing the Harlem Opera House, and it finally closed its doors in 1959.

▼▼▼

THE COTTON CLUB

In the fall of 1923 a swanky jazz supper club run by the Owney Madden crime syndicate opened its doors. The Cotton Club was sold to Madden by boxer Jack Johnson, who had operated the Club DeLuxe at that location from 1920 until 1922. Frequented by politicians, mobsters, journalists, and Broadway-show folks, the Cotton Club, which had a whites-only policy, offered its patrons extravagantly staged all-black revues with sexy chorus girls, hot jazz bands led by Duke Ellington, Cab Calloway, and Jimmy Lunceford, and bootlegged liquor. The Cotton Club was one of the most happening spots in Harlem along with Connie's Inn and Small's Paradise.

The opulent club boasted a lush interior with exotic jungle decor, potted palms, elegant draperies, and linen tablecloths. The multi-level room provided seating for 700. Tables were arranged in a horseshoe facing the small stage. The club's cover charge was $2.50, extra if you wanted a bottle of illegal booze. The menu featured steak, lobster, and shrimp as well as some soul food, Chinese, and Mexican dishes. Considered pricey in its day, a steak sandwich cost $1.25, a bowl of soup was fifty cents, and an entree of Moo Goo Gai Pan was $2.25.

The Madden Gang oversaw every aspect of the club, from hiring the band, songwriters, stage manager, costume and set designers, to auditioning the girls for the Cotton Club Chorus Line. Everyone who worked at the club understood that they were working for the Mob. The Madden Gang got around the Prohibition Law, which outlawed the sale of alcoholic beverages, by paying off the local police. In June 1925 their luck changed, when an FBI raid left the club padlocked and the owner and members of his gang under arrest for selling bootlegged liquor.

Owney Madden reopened the club three months later with a completely revamped revue. New sets, lighting, costumes, and a brand-new orchestra wowed the crowds. Duke Ellington and his

Washingtonians became the headliners in 1927, and the famous Cotton Club Chorus Line, made up of very light-skinned or "high yaller" black dancers, gyrated and moved to the beat of the band's jungle rhythms. Vaudeville acts, dancers, and blues singers filled out the bill. CBS radio did live broadcasts of Duke Ellington and his orchestra from the Cotton Club that put the club on the map. In 1928 Ellington asked the management to relax its whites-only policy, and they did so because his band was such a draw. Ellington and his band left the Cotton Club in 1931.

Cab Calloway and the Missourians replaced Ellington. Jimmie Lunceford and his orchestra succeeded the Calloway band in 1934. Some of the other talent that came through the Cotton Club included Lena Horne, Louis Armstrong, Ethel Waters, and Dorothy Dandridge. Hit songs that were first sung at the club included "Minnie the Moocher," "Stormy Weather," and "I've Got the World On A String."

The Cotton Club closed its doors on February 16, 1936. Whites felt that Harlem was not a safe place to party after the Harlem Riot of 1935, which caused business to fall off. The club reopened downtown later that year at 200 West 48th Street. The club finally closed for good in June 1940.

HOOFERS CLUB
2235 Seventh Avenue (1930–1945)

Located in the basement of the Lafayette Theatre, this was the spot where legendary dancers like Bill "Bojangles" Robinson, Honi Coles, Bunny Briggs, and Pete Nugent hung out.

LAFAYETTE THEATRE
2227 Seventh Avenue (1912–1964)

Originally a segregated theater, the 2,000-seat venue became famous for black theatrical productions. The Lafayette Players, a black theater company, performed revivals and Shakespearean plays with an all-black cast at the theater. The Lafayette also presented musical stage shows featuring performances by major black entertainers such as Ethel Waters, Bessie Smith, Bill "Bojangles" Robinson, Fletcher Henderson, Duke Ellington, and the Mills Brothers. The Tree of Hope, considered a good luck talisman for musicians and artists who rubbed the tree hoping to secure a gig, was located near the theater. Bill "Bojangles" Robinson reportedly placed a plaque on the Tree of Hope, immortalizing its legend for years to come. The tree was eventually cut down, and a sculpture was erected at 131st Street and Adam Clayton Powell Jr. Boulevard in 1972 to commemorate it. Today, Apollo Theatre amateur night hopefuls rub a stump of the Tree of Hope for good luck before their performances.

LINCOLN THEATRE
58 West 135th Street (1909–1964)

This 1,000-seat theater became the showcase for the Theatre Owner's Booking Agency (T.O.B.A.) productions. The agency was formed in 1920 to facilitate the booking of black productions into black theaters, especially in the South. A young Fats Waller played the organ for the silent films and vaudeville acts that also performed there. Bill "Count" Basie, who was even younger than Fats, watched Waller play the organ, no doubt soaking up some of his talent. The theater also presented performances by major talents of the time, including Duke Ellington, Ma Rainey, and Fletcher Henderson.

MINTON'S PLAYHOUSE
210 West 118th Street (1938–1964)

Formerly the dining room of the Cecil Hotel, the room was converted into a nightclub in 1938. Famous for its Monday night jam sessions, Minton's Playhouse is where Dizzy Gillespie and Thelonious Monk played bebop for the first time. There was some talk of actor Robert De Niro and a group of investors reviving the old club, but nothing has happened as of yet.

Renaissance Casino and Ballroom
150 West 138th Street (1915–1964)

The ballroom was the scene for all kinds of events, including dances, concerts, receptions, and basketball games featuring the New York Renaissance Basketball Team. Famous bands played at many of these events, as did the house band, which included well-known musicians Roy Eldridge, Cecil Scott, and Budd Johnson.

Pod's and Jerry's (Catagonia Club)
168 West 133rd Street (1925–1935)

This popular speakeasy, officially called the Catagonia Club, was known more familiarly by the owners' nicknames. After prohibition, the club was renovated to resemble a log cabin and the name was changed to the Log Cabin. Billie Holiday got her start here as a singer after she was turned down for a spot in the chorus line.

Savoy Ballroom
596 Lenox Avenue (1926–1958)

The battle of the bands, which included some of the best musicians from across the country, drew the crowds to this venue. One legendary jam-fest, with Fletcher Henderson and Chick Webb (representing the North) going up against King Oliver and 'Fess Williams (representing Chicago), caused traffic jams and packed the ballroom with hundreds of onlookers. Often referred to as the "home of the happy feet," the Savoy dancers created an array of steps including the Lindy Hop, Peckin,' Truckin,' Suzy Q, and the Congeroo.

ED SMALL'S PARADISE
2294 1/2 Seventh Avenue (1925–1964)

Considered the hottest spot in Harlem, this club had singing and dancing waiters, a musical revue, and a live radio broadcast of the band. This was one of the nightclubs the "slummers"—white partygoers looking for an evening of exotic happenings—from downtown frequented.

SMALL'S SUGAR CANE CLUB
2212 Fifth Avenue (1917–1925)

Owner Ed Small's waitstaff perfected the dancing waiter routine at his basement club before moving to the Seventh Avenue address. The Sugar Cane Club was one of the first clubs in Harlem to attract a white clientele. 'Sippi, a black cabdriver, would drive the white revelers uptown to party.

SHOPPING

Harlem is bursting at the seams with a wide variety of stores—big and small—to satisfy the shopper in all of us. The hub of the shopping district is located on West 125th Street from St. Nicholas Avenue to Frederick Douglass Boulevard, but do not confine yourself to just this area because there are wonderful shops throughout Harlem that are owned and operated by enterprising African and African American business folk. There are blocks and blocks of galleries, jewelry shops, African hairbraiding establishments, fabric stores, record shops, restaurants, clothing stores, and shoe stores offering all kinds of unique buys. What follows is a small sampling of the kinds of shopping destinations that are available to the visitor.

Malcolm Shabazz Harlem Market
Fifth Avenue (116th Street)
(212) 987-8131

This block-long tented bazaar, where African vendors sell everything from T-shirts, caps, and African art and artifacts, to sculpture, jewelry, and clothing, was originally located along the commercial hub of 125th Street. The marketplace was moved during Mayor Rudolph Giuliani's administration, amid protest from the vendors and local community activists. At its present location, busloads of tourists visit the market and purchase merchandise such as designer-like jeans, shirts, hats, and jackets at bargain prices. The market is open seven days a week from 10:00 A.M. to 8:30 P.M.

The Brownstone
2032 Fifth Avenue (between 125th and 126th Streets)
(212) 996-7980

A tri-level shopping experience that includes an apparel, accessories, cosmetics, and jewelry boutique on the first floor, a natural haircare salon on the second, and an African art gallery and gift shop, bridal salon, interior design service, and day spa on the third. After you've done your shopping you can relax over soup and a sandwich or some herbal tea and a slice of homemade cake at the cafe on level 3.

Open Wednesday through Saturday from 11:00 A.M. to 7:00 P.M. Major credit cards accepted.

Treasures of Egypt
Yaiqab Import & Export
2028 Fifth Avenue (between 125th and 126th Streets)
(212) 410-9357

Located virtually next door to The Brownstone, this exotic shop sells imported Egyptian art and perfumed oils, papyrus, natural haircare and body products such as shea butter, lotions, salts and gels, and incense.

Open Monday through Saturday from 10:00 A.M. to 10:00 P.M.; Sunday, from 11:00 A.M. to 7:00 P.M. Major credit cards accepted.

HARLEM UNDERGROUND
2027 Fifth Avenue (between 125th and 126th Streets)
(212) 987-9385

Across the street from Treasures of Egypt, Yaiqab Import & Export, this is a great place to get custom-made Harlem USA T-shirts, mugs, and caps. Many of the shirts and sweatshirts are embroidered on site.

Open Monday through Thursday from 10:00 A.M. to 7:00 P.M., Friday and Saturday from 10:00 A.M. to 8:00 P.M., and Sunday from Noon to 6:00 P.M. Major credit cards accepted.

ONE GOOD THING
Art & Soul Collectibles
367 Malcolm X Boulevard (between West 128th
   and West 129th Streets)
(646) 342-7389

An eclectic, tiny shop presenting contemporary fine artwork for under $500 and one-of-a-kind antiques, collectibles, objets d'art, as well as unique, custom-designed apparel, vintage clothing, and accessories. An intimate setting that looks more like someone's living room than a shop, everything is for sale at One Good Thing, so just ask.

Open Wednesday through Saturday from 11:00 A.M. to 7:00 P.M. and by appointment. Major credit cards accepted.

GRANDVIEW
2531 Frederick Douglass Boulevard (between West 135th
    and West 136th Streets)
(212) 694-7324

This beautiful shop of designer fashions for women sizes 2 to 22 is located in the historic Striver's Row neighborhood. The racks in the well-appointed store contain upscale, contemporary sportswear and casual attire from emerging black designers. The unique sweaters, tops, dresses, and slacks are made of beautiful fabrics in an array of colors and styles.

Open Tuesday through Saturday from Noon to 7:00 P.M., Sunday from 12:30 P.M. to 6:00 P.M. Major credit cards accepted.

THE HARLEM COLLECTIVE
2533 Frederick Douglass Boulevard (between West 135th
    and West 136th Streets)
(212) 368-0520

Right next door to Grandview, this lovely space offers unique artwork, one-of-a-kind clothing and artifacts, books, dolls, games, collectibles, gift items, and greeting cards. The Collective features the work of African American artisans, designers, and craftspeople.

Open Monday through Saturday from 11:00 A.M. to 7:00 P.M., Sunday from Noon to 5:00 P.M. Major credit cards accepted.

HARLEM MOTORSPORTS
200 West 140th Street (between Frederick Douglass and
    Adam Clayton Powell Jr. Boulevards)
(212) 234-5895

This is Harlem's first and only motorsport apparel, parts, and accessory shop. An authorized dealer of Vanson, NEXX, Davoucci, and Alpinestar leather goods, the store also has a wide selection of helmets. Known for its custom-painted designs on helmets and custom leather goods, Harlem Motorsports also stocks clothing for off-roaders. Open in the spring and summer, Monday through Saturday from 10:00 A.M. to 10:00 P.M., Sunday from Noon to 5:00 P.M. Open in the fall and winter, Tuesday through Friday, 10:00 A.M. to 7:00 P.M., Saturday from Noon to 8:00 P.M. Major credit cards accepted.

LIBERATION BOOKSTORE
421 Malcolm X Boulevard (West 131st Street)
(212) 281-4615

This legendary bookshop has been at the same location for over thirty-one years and is probably one of the oldest African American bookstores in New York State. The store specializes in books and periodicals about African, African American, Caribbean, and Latin American history and culture, including music, theater, language, and religion. The inventory is stocked with over forty categories of fiction, nonfiction, history, and biographies, including books by eighteenth-, nineteenth-, and twentieth-century writers. Also available is a selection of books for children from preschool to junior high school. Open Tuesday through Friday from 3:00 P.M. to 7:00 P.M. and on Saturday from Noon to 4:00 P.M.

THE SCARF LADY
408 Malcolm X Boulevard (between West 130th and West
   131st Streets)
(212) 862-7369

This popular store stocks over 500 imported and locally designed scarves in a variety of styles, including sarongs and beaded evening scarves. It also carries clothing by black designers Courtney Washington and Brenda Bey, as well as imported designer casual and dressy styles. Handcrafted jewelry and accessories by designer Audra Moore and hats by local designers Matthew and Helen are part of the unique inventory. Negro League memorabilia including shirts and caps are also in stock. The store sponsors workshops as well.

Open Tuesday through Saturday from 11:00 A.M. to 7:00 P.M. Call for more information.

HARLEM USA MALL
West 125th Street (at Frederick Douglass Boulevard)

This 275,00 square-foot retail space is the first state-of-the-art mall in Harlem. Opened in December 1999, the space houses The Disney Store, HMV Records, Old Navy, Modell's Sporting Goods, the Magic Johnson Theatre, New York Sports Clubs, and Chase Manhattan Bank.

BED AND BREAKFASTS

URBAN JEM GUEST HOUSE
2005 Fifth Avenue (between 124th and 125th Streets)
(212) 831-6029
www.urbanjem.com

This renovated 1878 brownstone in the Mount Morris Park Historic District is just steps away from the Marcus Garvey Memorial Park. It is also walking distance from the 125th Street shopping district, the Apollo Theatre, the National Black Theatre, and the Studio Museum in Harlem. Accommodations include two studio apartments with private kitchen and bath, a one-bedroom suite, and two furnished rooms with semi-private bath and kitchen. Air conditioning, in-room telephones, and cable TV are included in the rooms. A continental breakfast is available upon request and is included in the price. The parlor room looks out on Fifth Avenue and is used to host special events of interest to the community. Room rates range from $90 to $200 per night, minimum two-night stay. Call for information and reservations.

CRYSTAL'S CASTLE
119 West 119th Street (between Adam Clayton Powell Jr.
  and Malcolm X Boulevards)
(212) 865-5522
www.africanamericaninns.com

Located in the Mount Morris Park Historic District, this bed and breakfast is walking distance from the Studio Museum of Harlem, the Apollo Theatre, and a bunch of other great destinations in the Harlem community. Accommodations in the 100-year-old brownstone include two rooms with semi-private bath. Each room has a television and a small refrigerator. A common room and library are available for visitors to relax and read in. The continental breakfast menu offers a variety of choices with a decided Southern bent and is included in the price. Call for rates.

TOURS OF HARLEM

A LA CARTE NEW YORK TOURS
1270 Fifth Avenue
(212) 828-7360
www.hatt.org

This tour company offers escorted bus and walking tours of historic Harlem. The Sunday Church Gospel Tour begins with an inspirational service and exhilarating gospel singing at a historic Harlem church. Afterwards, tourists sample some down-home cooking at one of Harlem's delicious soul food restaurants. A special jazz tour features visits to the "lost shrines of jazz," and the Amateur Night at the Apollo excursion includes dinner at a soul food restaurant and a stop at the Apollo's own version of the *Gong Show*. The tours explore the culture and history of the legendary Harlem community. Call for meeting place, schedules, and prices.

BIG ONION WALKING TOURS
(212) 439-1090
www.bigonion.com

Big Onion's Historic Harlem walking tour explores the history, architecture, and people of Harlem. It includes visits to the historic Abyssinian Baptist Church, the meticulous homes of Striver's Row on West 138th and West 139th Streets, and other cultural sites such as those associated with Renaissance writers Zora Neale Hurston and Langston Hughes. The tour lasts approximately two hours. Group tours are available. Call for meeting place, schedule, and prices.

HARLEM SPIRITUALS
690 Eighth Avenue (between West 43rd and West 44th
   Streets)
(212) 391-7318
www.harlemspirituals.com

These multilingual bus tours in French, English, German, Italian, Spanish, and Portuguese offer visitors the chance to experience a soul-stirring Sunday service at a historic Harlem church, a jam session at a local jazz club, or a foot-stomping good time at a live gospel brunch. Harlem Spirituals also offers a tour of Harlem landmarks, which is topped off with a delicious lunch at a soul food restaurant.

Expert guides who know the history accompany all tours. Call for meeting place, schedule, and prices. Reservations required.

HARLEM, YOUR WAY! TOURS UNLIMITED

129 West 130th Street (between Malcom X and Adam
  Clayton Powell Jr. Boulevards)
(212) 690-1687
www.harlemyourwaytours.com

Harlem, Your Way! has been providing Harlem sights and sounds through its walking and bus tours since 1982. The company, which is based in Harlem, offers a Sunday Gospel Tour, a Wednesday Night Champagne Safari to *Amateur Night at the Apollo*, and a Champagne Jazz Safari to the hot nightspots. These are just a few of the packages available to visitors wanting to experience both the history and the present culture of Harlem. You can even plan your own tour with the assistance of one of the Harlem, Your Way! tour experts. Call for meeting place, schedule, and prices.

HARLEM HERITAGE TOURS

230 West 116th Street—Suite 3C (between Malcolm X
  and Adam Clayton Powell Jr. Boulevards)
(212) 280-7888

This company specializes in tours of Harlem that celebrate the history and culture of the community. The tours, conducted by people who actually live in Harlem, explore the music, food, heritage, and art of the area. Walking tours and bus tours are available. Call for meeting place, schedules, and prices.

JOYCE GOLD HISTORY TOURS OF NEW YORK

(212) 242-5762
www.nyctours.com

Joyce Gold's Vital Heart of Harlem: Its Spirit and Substance tour is chock-full of anecdotal information presented in a fun way. She covers the history of Harlem from its days as a farming community in the early seventeenth century, through the Jazz Age and the Harlem Renaissance in the 1920s and 1930s, to the present day. Private tours are available. Call for meeting place, schedules, and prices.

BROOKLYN

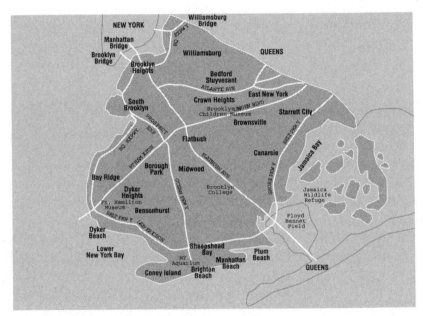

Courtesy of Harlem Spirituals, Gospel & Jazz Tours, Inc.

3

Brooklyn

HISTORY OF BROOKLYN

The Dutch West India Company settled Brooklyn in 1635. The rich, fertile farmlands and the natural harbor were major attractions for the settlers who occupied the area with their Indian neighbors, the Lenapes and the Delawareans. Breukelyn (Brooklyn), New Amersfoort (Flatlands), Midwout (Flatbush), New Utrecht, and Boswick (Bushwick) were chartered as separate towns over a ten-year period, beginning in 1646. The English established Gravesend during this same period.

When the British took over from the Dutch in 1664, they imported African slaves and indentured servants to farm the land. Ferry service, which was implemented in the 1640s, transported the farmers' produce to the markets in Manhattan. Kings County was established in 1683 to facilitate the collection of taxes, the subdivision of land, and the creation of roads. Brooklyn prospered and became the largest slave-holding county in New York State.

In the summer of 1776, Kings County was the site of the Battle of Long Island in which the Continental Army, led by George Washington, was defeated. The British occupied Brooklyn for seven years, warehousing thousands of war prisoners on ships docked in Wallabout Bay, now known as the Brooklyn Navy Yard.

At the turn of the century Brooklyn was the only town in Kings County that had steady economic growth. Its downtown location, close to the ferry, was a major factor in the creation of new businesses and the increase in population. With the invention of Robert Fulton's steam ferry in 1814, Brooklyn became the world's first commuter suburb. Manhattan businessmen and their families flocked to Brooklyn Heights, an easy commute to lower Manhattan. The town became a village in 1816 and elected its own officials; in 1834 Brooklyn became a city.

After slaves were emancipated in New York State in 1827, several all-black communities sprang up in Brooklyn. Weeksville and Carrville in Central Brooklyn (Bedford-Stuyvesant) and Crow Hill (Crown Heights) were settled by free blacks who worked on farms and as fishermen. Not much is known about Carrville and Crow Hill except that these communities were part of property purchased in the 1830s by black landowners William Thomas, Henry C. Thompson, and Samuel Anderson.

Weeksville was named for James Weeks, a free black man who purchased land from the Lefferts family in 1838. Weeks migrated from Virginia and worked as a stevedore at South Street Seaport in Manhattan. His home was located at the corner of Schenectady and Atlantic Avenues. The population increased in all of the black settlements when blacks fleeing from the Draft Riots of 1863 in Manhattan sought refuge in Weeksville and the surrounding communities. The four wood-frame nineteenth-century houses at 1698–1708 Bergen Street are the only homes left of the Weeksville community. Designated as New York City landmarks and listed in the National Register of Historic Places, the properties, which are situated on the historic Hunterfly Road, are now owned by the Society for the Preservation of Weeksville and Bedford-Stuyvesant History.

Many black institutions and organizations were founded in Weeksville. Churches, schools, and social organizations were all part of this burgeoning community. The Bethel Tabernacle A.M.E. Church, founded in 1847 at the corner of Schenectady and Dean Streets, was the first black church in Weeksville. It is now located across the street from its original site. Berean Missionary Baptist Church, located on Prospect Place between Utica and Rochester Avenues, moved in 1894 to its current address on Bergen Street, down the street from the Weeksville Houses. Among the earliest churches in Weeksville, Berean Missionary Baptist Church was established in the late 1880s. Colored School #2 opened in 1853 to serve the children of Weeksville and was located at the corner of Dean Street and Troy Avenue. Public School 243, which was renamed the Weeksville School in 1975, is on that same site and today continues the legacy of Weeksville. The African Civilization Society on Dean Street published *Freedman's Torchlight*, a Weeksville newspaper. The *Torchlight*, a monthly, had articles about black self-help and information about the Freedman's Schools, where former slaves could be educated. It also supplied lessons in basic English, arithmetic, and geography on its front pages, which were used as a textbook by its black readers.

Two prominent African Americans who lived in Weeksville were Dr. Susan Smith, the first black woman to graduate from medical school in 1870, and Moses P. Cobb, one of the first black policemen in Brooklyn. Dr. Smith was the co-founder of the Women's Hospital and Dispensary at Myrtle and Grand Avenues, which moved to 808 Prospect Place and was renamed the Memorial Hospital for Women and Children. Mr. Cobb, born a slave, came to New York from North Carolina. He joined the police force in 1892 after working on the waterfront. Another black police officer in Brooklyn was Wiley Overton. He served on the force from 1891 to 1892.

The Society for the Preservation of Weeksville and Bedford-Stuyvesant History has restored the buildings at 1698–1708 Bergen Street as the Weeksville African-American Museum, which houses exhibits about the early community. The Society believes that "knowledge of our culture, heritage, and our contribution to this nation will help all of us, especially our children."

Brooklyn became a borough of New York City in 1898. Its eighty-one square miles, which include the predominately black neighborhoods of Bedford-Stuyvesant, Fort Greene, East Flatbush, and Crown Heights, have a population of 2,465,326, including 898,350 black residents (according to the 2000 census). Brooklyn has the largest Caribbean community in the United States. Eastern Parkway is the site of the annual West Indian Day Festival, which takes place over the Labor Day weekend (see page 212). Throngs of people come to the festival to experience Caribbean culture, watch the parade of colorful floats and costumed dancers, eat the spicy food, and listen to the music.

BROOKLYN ITINERARY

Unlike Manhattan, this borough's links to the history of black New York is a little more difficult to ferret out. Many of the sites of significance to African American history are not located near subway lines, making it difficult to travel on one's own. The best way to see the historic areas of black Brooklyn is on a guided bus tour. The Braggin' About Brooklyn Tour starts in downtown Brooklyn at the building where Jackie Robinson signed his baseball contract and made sports history by becoming the first African American to play major league baseball. The tour then travels to Brooklyn Heights, the first commuter suburb of New York City, and to Plymouth Church of the Pilgrims at 75 Hicks Street, where abolitionist Henry Ward Beecher was the pastor from 1847 to 1887. It is believed that the church, called the Grand Central Terminal of the Underground Railroad, was a refuge for fugitive slaves who hid in the tunnels beneath the church. (See tour information on page 169.)

From Brooklyn Heights the tour travels to Central Brooklyn, where there were several communities of free blacks such as Carrville, Crow Hill, and Weeksville, which is the only one that

The Weeksville Houses, on Bergen Street in Brooklyn (Photo by Linda Tarrant-Reid)

remains. The nineteenth-century wood frame houses at 1698–1708 Bergen Street in Bedford-Stuyvesant only hint at the history. Hunterfly Road, the small curved road in front of the homes, predates the Revolutionary War and is believed to have been the road George Washington and his troops used to travel to the ill-fated Battle of Long Island. (See History of Brooklyn, pages 145 to 148.)

The Weeksville Houses are down the street from the historic Berean Missionary Baptist Church, one of the oldest black churches in Brooklyn, at 1635 Bergen Street. Also in the Bedford-Stuyvesant neighborhood is Bedford-Stuyvesant Restoration's Skylight Gallery, and the Billie Holiday Theater at 1368 Fulton Street. The Simmons Collection African Arts Museum, located at 1063 Fulton Street at Classon Avenue, has an extensive collection of traditional and contemporary African art and is worth a visit.

The Fort Greene community, where film director Spike Lee lived for many years (See sidebar on page 159), is a destination

The Weeksville Lady—the symbol of the Society for the Preservation of Weeksville and Bedford-Stuyvesant History—is an image from an early tintype found during an archeological dig at Weeksville. (Photo courtesy of the Society for the Preservation of Weeksville and Bedford-Stuyvesant)

within itself. The shopping district between South Elliott Street and South Oxford Street is a great place to spend the day. The tiny area is crammed with clothing stores, restaurants, and small specialty stores stocked with goodies. Start at the 4W Circle of Art and Enterprise at 704 Fulton Street and browse the diverse inventory of Afro-fused clothing, Afrocentric cards and gifts, cosmetics, and books. Down the street, visit the Courtney Washington Fashion Studio (674 Fulton Street) where racks of beautifully designed dresses, shirts, and pants in simple, elegant fabrics are on display. If shopping makes you hungry, the area offers a variety of food choices from healthy food at the Sunshine Cafe at 662 Fulton Street, to nouvelle soul at the comfy Brooklyn Moon Cafe at 745 Fulton Street.

HISTORIC SITES AND LANDMARKS

SOCIETY FOR THE PRESERVATION OF WEEKSVILLE
AND BEDFORD-STUYVESANT HISTORY
(Hunterfly Road Historic Houses District of Weeksville)
1698–1708 Bergen Street (between Buffalo and
  Rochester Avenues)
(718) 756-5250

The wood-framed houses that date from 1840 to 1883 and a hint of a colonial road are the visible signs of existence of the black community of Weeksville established in 1838. The impetus to know more about the long-forgotten free-black settlement came from two students who were taking a neighborhood history workshop at Pratt Institute. They wanted to find out if the stories they had heard about Weeksville from older black Brooklynites were true. Their research led them to the rundown houses on Bergen Street, across from a Bedford-Stuyvesant housing project. The importance of their find was reaffirmed when their instructor and a pilot flew over the area and spotted a road that ran in front of the houses. They later learned that the road, known as Hunterfly Road, was the one that General George Washington and his men took on their way to the Battle of Long Island. According to a Kings County map and a record of Hunterfly Road, it was originally an Indian trail leading to wampum beds on the shores of Jamaica Bay in the mid-1600s. (Wampum was the currency used by the Indians to purchase goods.)

The community of Weeksville was named for James Weeks, a free black man from Virginia who purchased the land from the estate of Leffert Lefferts. Weeks worked as a stevedore on the docks around what is now South Street Seaport in Manhattan.

Eventually other free blacks bought land in the surrounding area and the community of Weeksville grew. Although a poor community, it had its own school, several churches, and a newspaper. Colored School #2 opened in 1853 (at Dean Street and Troy Avenue), and was started to educate the children of Weeksville. Today, the Weeksville School, P.S. 243, stands on that site. The Bethel Tabernacle A.M.E. Church, organized in 1847 at the corner of Schenectady Avenue and Dean Street, was the first black church in Weeksville. *Freedman's Torchlight*, Weeksville's newspaper, was published by the African Civilization Society and edited by Rev. Rufus Perry in 1866. Former slaves who were learning to read and write used the front page of the newspaper as a textbook.

The Draft Riots of 1863 brought to Brooklyn blacks fleeing Manhattan because of beatings, lynchings, and burnings by angry white mobs resentful of being drafted into the Civil War. Many of these new arrivals sought shelter not only in Weeksville, but also in the black settlements of Carrville and Crow Hill (which is now Crown Heights) in Central Brooklyn.

The Weeksville Society Historical Museum, located at the Bergen Street address, includes several period rooms with artifacts from Weeksville, archeology, restoration, and audio-visual exhibits, and a storytelling garden for young people. The museum is open Monday through Friday. Admission is suggested. Call for more information.

THE BROOKLYN HOWARD COLORED ORPHAN ASYLUM SITE

Formerly the Home for Freed Children and Others, the orphan asylum was originally located at Pacific Street and Ralph Avenue. The home later moved to Troy Avenue and Dean Street, which is now the site of the Transit Authority Depot. Mrs. S. A. Tillman, a black woman, established it as a shelter for homeless black children in 1866. She saw the need to create an environment for children whose parents had either died or were working in service and could not take care of them.

THE ZION HOME FOR COLORED AGED SITE

This home was located next door to the Howard Colored Orphanage on Dean Street and was founded in 1869 by the Zion African Methodist Episcopal Church in Manhattan as a home for elderly poor. After experiencing many difficulties because of a lack of funding, the King's Daughters (a white organization) and the members of the Concord Baptist Church helped to purchase a building at 1888 Atlantic Avenue. The home was later moved to a new building at St. John's Place and Kingston Avenue, where it was renamed the Brooklyn Home for the Aged in 1954.

BEREAN MISSIONARY BAPTIST CHURCH
1635 Bergen Street (between Utica and Rochester Avenues)
(718) 774-0466; (718) 778-5797

One of the earliest churches established in the Weeksville community. It moved from its original site on Prospect Place to the Bergen Street site in 1894. The church members provided clothing and food to fugitive slaves on the Underground Railroad.

ST. PHILLIP'S CHURCH
MacDonough Street (between Stuyvesant and Lewis Avenues)

Founded in 1904 at 1610 Dean Street, this was where the first Black company of the United Boys Brigade of America (an early incarnation of the Boy Scouts) began. The church moved to its present site on MacDonough Street in 1944.

BRIDGE STREET AFRICAN WESLEYAN METHODIST EPISCOPAL CHURCH
277 Stuyvesant Avenue (between Jefferson Avenue
   and Hancock Street)
(718) 452-3936

Established in 1818, this is the oldest black church in Brooklyn. The church was located at 311 Bridge Street in downtown Brooklyn before it moved to Bedford-Stuyvesant in 1938. It is believed that the church was a stop on the Underground Railroad.

SILOAM PRESBYTERIAN CHURCH
260 Jefferson Avenue (between Marcy
  and Nostrand Avenues)
(718) 789-7050

Founded in 1847, this church was also a stop on the Underground Railroad.

PLYMOUTH CHURCH OF THE PILGRIMS
75 Hicks Street (between Cranberry and Orange Streets)
(718) 624-4743
www.plymouthchurch.org

Reformer and abolitionist Henry Ward Beecher, brother of *Uncle Tom's Cabin* author Harriet Beecher Stowe, preached from this pulpit. Built in 1850, this historic congregational church, which was originally two churches, was also visited by Abraham Lincoln in 1860. The sanctuary was for many years the largest public building in Brooklyn. Speakers of note have included Booker T. Washington and Martin Luther King Jr. Known as the Grand Central Terminal of the Underground Railroad, Plymouth Church has a series of tunnels that was purportedly used by fugitive slaves. A designated National Historic Landmark, the church seats 2,000. Tours are available after service on Sunday.

JACKIE ROBINSON RESIDENCE
5224 Tilden Avenue

Located in the East Flatbush section of Brooklyn, this was the home of baseball great Jackie Robinson from 1948 to 1949. Robinson broke the color barrier when he became the first black to play major league baseball in 1947. That same year, the Dodgers won the pennant. Robinson was voted the National League's Most

Valuable Player in 1949. Although designated a national historic landmark, this is a private residence and is not open to the public.

MUSEUMS AND GALLERIES

SIMMONS COLLECTION AFRICAN ARTS MUSEUM
1063 Fulton Street (at Classon Avenue)
(718) 230-0933

This Bedford-Stuyvesant museum's collection contains traditional and contemporary African art consisting of paintings, masks, statuary, musical instruments, jewelry, tapestries, and artifacts. Founder, director, and curator Stanfield Simmons acquired the collection during his extensive travels throughout western, central, and eastern Africa. The museum offers lectures and slide presentations to groups, including students, seniors, and church groups. The museum also organizes guided tours to Africa, South America, and India. The museum gift shop sells African sculptures, handicrafts, jewelry, and clothing.

Open Wednesday, Saturday, and Sunday. Call for more information.

BEDFORD-STUYVESANT RESTORATION CORPORATION
Center for Art and Culture
Skylight Gallery
1368 Fulton Street (between New York and Brooklyn Avenues)
(718) 636-6976

The exhibits in this 3,000-square-foot space feature contemporary artists of the African diaspora. African American, South African, Caribbean, Brazilian, and Guyanese painters, sculptors, collagists, photographers, and folk artists all make up this international gallery. Open from 11 A.M. to 7 P.M. Tuesday through Friday and from 11 A.M. to 5 P.M. on Saturday. Call for more information.

Brooklyn Museum of Art
200 Eastern Parkway (at Washington Avenue)
(718) 638-5000

The museum's permanent collection includes the Arts of Africa exhibit, which features works from central Africa. The exhibit is one of the largest and most important assemblages of African art in the country. The galleries where the African collections are housed were recently expanded and reinstalled with 250 works of art, including a carved ivory gong from the Edo people of Benin, and an eighteenth-century wooden figure of the King of the Kuba people of Zaire. The exhibit also has masks, statues, jewelry, and household objects on display. The museum shops and cafe are open during museum hours.

Open Wednesday through Sunday. On First Night, the first Saturday night of every month, the museum is free and is open until 11 P.M. Group tours are available. Admission: $4; $2 students with I.D.; $1.50 seniors. Free admission for kids under twelve (with an adult) and members.

Brooklyn's History Museum at the Brooklyn Historical Society
128 Pierrepont Street
(718) 254-9830
www.brooklynhistory.org

Located at the Brooklyn Historical Society, the museum has more than 1,000 artifacts, memorabilia, furniture pieces, paintings, prints, and photographs commemorating Brooklyn's long history. Its permanent collection includes works related to the Brooklyn Bridge, Coney Island, the Brooklyn Navy Yard, and the Brooklyn Dodgers. The museum sponsors family events, presentations, and workshops, and has hands-on programs for school and youth groups that emphasize the cultural diversity of the borough.

The museum is closed for restoration and will reopen in 2001. Call for more information or visit their Web site.

THE BROOKLYN HISTORICAL SOCIETY
128 Pierrepont Street
(718) 254-9830
www.brooklynhistory.org.

Founded in 1863, the Society's research library, museum, and education center offers services and programs that reflect the rich heritage of the diverse cultures of Brooklyn, past and present. The
Society's collection includes over 9,000 pieces, including prints,
drawings, broadsides, watercolors, paintings, artifacts, clothing, furniture, and other memorabilia. As of this writing, the building is
undergoing a major restoration that will include the construction
of a new History Discovery Center for educational programs.
Areas of the historical society and the museum are not accessible
to the public during the renovation project scheduled for comple-
tion in 2001. Call for more information.

LEFFERTS HOMESTEAD AND CHILDREN'S MUSEUM
Prospect Park (at Flatbush Avenue and Empire
  Boulevard)
(718) 965-6505

The homestead, located in Prospect Park, is an eighteenth-
century two-story building that is now a children's museum offering a look at life in colonial Brooklyn. The landowning Lefferts
family sold land to free black James Weeks—which later became
known as the black community of Weeksville.

Open Thursday through Sunday. Call for more information.

LEWIS GALLERY
525 Atlantic Avenue (between Third and Fourth Avenues)
(718) 624-8372

Located on Antique Row, a neighborhood chock-full of small collectibles shops, this gallery features the work of artists of color
from America, Africa, Guam, and the Caribbean. The collection
includes oils and pastels by Al Lewis, a Brooklyn-born multimedia

artist, oil and acrylic paintings by Frank Morrison, and serigraphs and silkscreens by Charles Bibbs. Black memorabilia, collectible figurines, and handmade dolls are also exhibited. The tri-level space opens onto the main gallery, with the museum shop on the lower level and custom framing on the upper level. The gallery hosts several art shows throughout the year. Workshops in quilt-making, doll-making, and wreath-making are also available.

Open seven days a week (except in the summer, when it is closed Sunday).

CLINTON HILL SIMPLY ART GALLERY
583 Myrtle Avenue (between Classon Avenue and Taaffe
   Place)
(718) 857-0074

Specializing in works on paper, this gallery's ethnic art reflects the culture and lifestyles of African Americans, Caribbeans, and His-panics. The collection includes paintings, photographs, and sculp-tures. Simply Art presents revolving exhibits by emerging and local artists every month in Gallery Too. Call for more information.

CULTURAL CENTERS

BILLIE HOLIDAY THEATRE
Bedford-Stuyvesant Restoration Corporation
1368 Fulton Street (between New York and Brooklyn
   Avenues)
(718) 636-0918

A community-based cultural arts institution for over twenty-five years, the Billie Holiday Theatre is home to an award-winning the-ater company in the heart of Bedford-Stuyvesant. The company produces original works by African Americans that inspire, edu-cate, and entertain—it is often considered training ground for

▼

SPIKE LEE

Filmmaker, super Knick basketball fan, and Nike pitchman. Spike Lee wears each of these hats, but to many Brooklyn residents, especially in the Fort Lee section, he was a neighbor and documentarian of life in this crowded and diverse borough. Spike's production company, 40 Acres and a Mule Filmworks, is still in Brooklyn, but he now lives with his family in Manhattan.

Spike Lee was born in Atlanta, Georgia, on March 20, 1957. His father, a composer-musician, and mother, an art and literature teacher, later moved the family to Brooklyn. Lee, the oldest of five, has set several of his films in his adopted home. *She's Gotta Have It* (1986), Lee's first feature, opens at the Williamsburg, Brooklyn, loft of lead character Nola Darling. *Do the Right Thing* (1989), his seminal work on race relations, is set in Bedford-Stuyvesant. And *Crooklyn* (1994), the semi-autobiographical film about a family coping with the loss of their mother to cancer, is set in Cobble Hill.

Lee completed his undergraduate work at his family's alma mater, Atlanta's Morehouse College. He received an M.F.A. in film production from New York University's Tisch School of the Arts. His student film *Joe's Barbershop: We Cut Heads* was shown on PBS.

Using a repertory approach, Lee employs a stable of actors and technicians from film to film. Lee's sister Joie, an actress, his brother David, a photographer, and his father, Bill, a musician-composer, have all worked on his films. The siblings even collaborated on *Crooklyn*. Spike Lee's other films include: *School Daze* (1988), *Mo' Better Blues* (1990), *Jungle Fever* (1991), *Malcolm X* (1992), *Clockers* (1995), *Girl Six* (1996), *Get On the Bus* (1996), *Summer of Sam* (1999), The original *Kings of Comedy* (2000), and *Bamboozled* (2000).

◆

aspiring theatre professionals. The Billie Holiday Theatre has nurtured the careers of many performers, including actor Samuel L. Jackson, choreographer Debbie Allen, and producer Samm-Art Williams. The theatre has produced many hit shows, including *Inacent Black and the Five Brothers,* which went to Broadway and starred Melba Moore, the musical *Over Forty*; and the hit comedy *Lotto.* Call for a performance schedule.

BROOKLYN ACADEMY OF MUSIC
30 Lafayette Avenue (at Ashland Place)
(718) 636-4100

This major Brooklyn cultural arts institution presents many events throughout the year that reflect Brooklyn's diverse community. The Academy hosts performances featuring dance, music, and other arts from a range of disciplines and cultures. Two annual events highlighting the contributions of African Americans are the Martin Luther King Jr. Commemoration in January, which honors the slain civil rights activist's achievements, and DanceAfrica, a festival of dance and music in June. Call for a performance schedule.

DINING OUT

AKWAABA CAFE
393 Lewis Avenue (at MacDonough Street)
(718) 774-1444

In Akan, a Ghanian dialect, *akwaaba* means welcome, an appropriate name for this elegant and warm corner restaurant in historic Stuyvesant Heights. The owners also run the stunning bed and breakfast up the block on MacDonough Street, the Akwaaba Mansion. Serving African diaspora dishes and American cuisine, guests feast on Cornbread-Battered Calamari with Marinara Sauce, Pan-Fried Crab Cake with a Remoulade Sauce, and Spicy

Garlic Shrimp for starters. Entrees run the gamut, from Rosemary-Rubbed Grilled Sirloin with Garlic Mashed Potatoes and Vegetables, to Southern Fried Chicken with Macaroni and Cheese and Collard Greens. Sunday Brunch is a must at this airy and well-appointed bistro. Akwaaba also hosts an exciting array of events such as Literary Night on Thursday, where poets and best-selling authors read from their work. There is also a gift shop that sells cards, T-shirts, caps, and books.

Open from Thursday to Sunday for dinner; Brunch served on Sunday. Call for reservations. (See page 165.)

PORK KNOCKERS
956 Atlantic Avenue (between Washington
   and Grand Avenues)
(718) 638-0727

Jamaican delicacies are served at this Bedford-Stuyvesant eatery, including Jerk Chicken Wings, Coconut Shrimp, Curried Chicken, and a variety of fish dishes. Eat in or take out.

Open seven days a week. Major credit cards accepted. (See page 164.)

FORT GREENE
Butta'cup Lounge
271 Adelphi Street (at Dekalb Avenue)
(718) 522-1669

This bi-level brownstone with 50s- and 60s-style furnishings caters to the hip elite of Brooklyn. The menu is a melange of Caribbean, Asian, and soul dishes as well as a variety of seafood and vegetarian offerings. One whimsical starter is the Butta' Box for two which includes Beef Sate, Fried Wonton, Spring Roll, and Pepper Shrimp. Entrees including the Caribbean Chicken Salad, Lil' Big Daddy's Fried Chicken, and the Coconut Crusted Salmon with Carrot Guava Sauce are all palate pleasers. Open Tuesday through

Saturday for breakfast, lunch and dinner. Also serves Brunch and dinner on Sunday. Major credit cards accepted.

Two Steps Down
240 Dekalb Avenue (Clermont and Vanderbilt Avenues)
(718) 399-2020

Specializing in Southern and Caribbean cuisines, this Fort Greene restaurant's menu puts the emphasis on seafood. Salmon and red snapper dishes, as well as Fried or Jerk Chicken, Barbecue Spareribs, and Grilled Steak are delectable entree choices.

Open Wednesday through Sunday for dinner and Brunch on Sunday. Major credit cards accepted.

Sol
229 Dekalb Avenue (Clermont and Dekalb Avenues)
(718) 222-1510

This stylishly appointed restaurant and bar in the Fort Greene section offers regional cuisine from Latin America. Some unique menu selections include Pressed Cuban Sandwich with Ginger Orange Pork, Sol Fish and Chips, and Salmon Tempura with Honey Teriyaki Sauce and Cilantro Fries. Vegetarians and fish lovers have an assortment of dishes to choose from.

Open seven days a week for dinner; Brunch served on Sunday. Major credit cards accepted.

Keur n' Deye
737 Fulton Street (between South Elliott Place
and South Portland Street)
(718) 875-4937

Also in the historic Fort Greene section, this African restaurant offers traditional Senegalese homestyle cooking. The national dish of Senegal, *Tiébu Dieun*—a fish stew in a rich tomato sauce with seasonal vegetables—is served with rice. *Yassa*, from the southern region, is a dish of marinated chicken, fish, or beef broiled or fried in a lemon sauce with onion and peppers; it is served with rice or couscous. Other delectable offerings are Shrimp in Okra Sauce, Curry Chicken, and Oxtail Stew. Vegetarians can feast on Okra in Tomato and Onion Sauce or Fresh Vegetables in a Tomato Sauce. Desserts are homemade. The Sweet Potato Pie, Carrot Cake, Coconut Pecan Pie, and the Coconut Cream Cake are all good choices.

Open Tuesday through Sunday for lunch and dinner.

BROOKLYN MOON CAFE
745 Fulton Street (between South Elliott Place
   and South Portland Street)
(718) 243-0424

A cozy, comfortable cafe with overstuffed, upholstered chairs and settees and a gentle ambience make it very difficult for the owner to turn over these tables. Diners sit, chat, and relax over some scrumptious dishes. Serving lunch and dinner, this little gem also has a fabulous Saturday and Sunday Brunch with entrees of Banana, Strawberry, and Apple Pancakes Served with Strawberry or Cinnamon Butter; Feta, Spinach, or Smoked Salmon Omelette; Salmon Croquettes, and Southern Fried Chicken. All platters come with a choice of sides, including Turkey Bacon, Sausage, Grits, Home Fries, Seasonal Fresh Fruit, and Mango Avocado Salad. The dinner menu includes Oven-Roasted Chicken, Fried Whiting with Green Curry Sauce, and Grilled Salmon entrees. Pasta lovers can choose between the Linguini with Roasted Eggplant in Marinara Sauce, Vegetable Lasagna, and Farfalle Pasta with Shrimp in Lemon Butter Sauce.

Open Tuesday through Sunday for lunch and dinner.

SUNSHINE CAFE
662 Fulton Street (South Elliot Place)
(718) 222-1705

This tiny restaurant offers a healthy menu of gourmet salads, chicken and vegetable wraps, and sandwiches. Freshly squeezed juices like orange, carrot, and apple, as well as vegiblends of parsley, carrot, and ginger are also very popular. Fruit smoothies made with the freshest ingredients will quench your thirst after you've been shopping on Fulton Street's dynamic retail strip. Gourmet coffee paired with Homemade Apple Spice Cake, Cheesecake, Chocolate Cake, Banana Walnut Loaf, or a Yogurt Muffin is a winning combination.

Open seven days a week.

JOLOFF RESTAURANT
930 Fulton Street (St. James Street)
(718) 636-4011

This popular spot offers traditional West African cuisine, and specializes in Senegalese cooking. *Boulette* (fish balls), *Pastels* (fish patties), Vegetarian *Pastels*, and Plantains are just a few of the appetizers on the menu. Entrees of fish, poultry, and beef feature Red Snapper with Onion Sauce, French Fries, and Salad, and Lamb Stewed in Peanut Butter Sauce with Ground Okra and Rice—all are a great introduction to this wonderful cuisine.

Open seven days a week for lunch and dinner.

LIVE MUSIC

PORK KNOCKERS
956 Atlantic Avenue (between Washington and Grand
  Avenues)
(718) 638-0727

This club-restaurant offers live jazz, Caribbean, and Latin music on Wednesday, Thursday, and Friday. On Mondays revelers belt out karaoke. In the summer, the music is taken outside to the outdoor bar and patio. Call for more information. (See page 161.)

AKWAABA CAFE
393 Lewis Ave. (at MacDonough St.)
(718) 774-1444

This restaurant serves up live Jazz on Saturday with a buffet dinner. Call for more information. (See page 160.)

SISTAS' PLACE COFFEE HOUSE
456 Nostrand Avenue (at Jefferson Avenue)
(718) 398-1766

A community gathering place where one can sip herbal tea or coffee and listen to live jazz, poetry readings, and hip-hop artists who show their stuff at the open-mic night. "Conversations," a series of discussions between audience members and artists, takes place on the first and third Sunday of each month. Call for a performance/event schedule.

SHOPPING

FULTON MALL
Fulton Street (between Flatbush Avenue
   and Adams Street)
(718) 852-5118

The Fulton Mall is an eight-block urban street mall located in Downtown Brooklyn between Adams Street and Flatbush Avenue. The Mall contains more than 200 stores, including Macy's, The Children's Place, Dr. Jay's for Women, Baker Shoes, Lane Bryant, Modell's Sporting Goods, Nobody Beats the Wiz, Payless Shoes, Strawberry, The Avenue, Toys R' Us, and more.
   Open seven days a week.

4 W CIRCLE OF ART & ENTERPRISE
704 Fulton Street (between South Oxford and South
   Portland Streets)
(718) 875-6500

This retail cooperative in the Fort Greene section of Brooklyn was established in 1991 to allow home-based businesses to move into a retail space at minimal risk. The cooperative sublets space to vendors and provides business counseling services, administrative support, and shared sales staff. Currently, there are five businesses at 4W Circle of Art and Enterprise: the Eden Collection, which sells clothing and accessories for career woman of color; Tamu, a hair-accessory company that sells hair care products and ornaments for natural hairstyles; Simple Pleasures, a gift shop that features Afrocentric greeting cards and gifts; Tribal Truths, which sells a line of Afrofused clothing; and Miksu Cosmetics, a cosmetics line for all women.

   Open Tuesday through Sunday.

MOSHOOD
698 Fulton Street (Between South Oxford and South
   Portland Streets)
(718) 243-9433
www.afrikanspirit.com

A unique clothing store in the Fort Greene neighborhood, that features the fashions of Nigerian-born owner-designer Moshood. The clothing combines traditional Afrikan tailoring with a western flavor. The slogan "Wear Moshood, Wear Yourself" speaks to the cultural imprint the designer is imparting with his work. A second store is located in Atlanta, Georgia.

   Open Monday through Sunday.

COURTNEY WASHINGTON FASHION STUDIO
674 Fulton Street (between South Elliott Place and South
   Oxford Street)
(718) 852-6899

The spare but elegant studio of clothes designer Courtney Washington is located right in the Fort Greene hub. Mr. Washington designs for men and women, and his collection includes drawstring pants, simple, loose-fitting tops, dresses, and evening gowns. The clothing is made out of linen, cotton, and other natural fibers.
   Open Monday through Saturday.

F.U.L.A.N.Y. F.A.S.H.I.O.N. INC.
700 Fulton Street (between South Oxford and South
   Portland Streets)
(718) 246-3777; (718) 246-4004

This custom-tailoring and retail store offerings include unique suits, dresses, skirts, evening wear, and clothes for all occasions for men and women.
   Open Monday through Saturday.

CAROL'S DAUGHTER
One South Elliott Place (at DeKalb Avenue)
(718) 596-1862
www.carolsdaughter.com

Featured in *Essence Magazine*, this outlet offers a full line of soothing personal care products for face, hair, feet, and the entire body. The extensive line includes products such as Healthy Hair Butter, Mimosa Hair Honey, Mango Body Butter, and Peppermint Foot Lotion. To place an order, call the toll free number: (877) 540-2101.
   Open Monday through Sunday.

Bedford-Stuyvesant brownstones in Brooklyn. (Photo by Linda Tarrant-Reid)

AFRICAN PEOPLE'S FARMERS' MARKET
456 Nostrand Avenue (at Jefferson Avenue)
(718) 398-1766

This community farmers' market is only open on the weekends. Fresh fruits, vegetables, and a variety of juices are available at reasonable prices. The market also sponsors education programs on preventive health care for the community. Call for more information.

ZAWADI GIFT SHOP
519 Atlantic Avenue (Between Third and Fourth Avenues)
(718) 624-7822

Located in downtown Brooklyn on historic Antique Row, this unique gift shop has an inventory with a little bit of everything: ethnic jewelry, art, and artifacts; housewares; handmade black figurines, including Thomas Blackshear figurines, dolls, and collectibles; and all kinds of unusual gifts. Custom framing is also available.

Open Tuesday through Sunday.

BED AND BREAKFASTS

AKWAABA MANSION
347 MacDonough Street (between Stuyvesant and Lewis
  Avenues)
(718) 455-5958

This restored 1860s Italianate villa featuring eighteen rooms with exquisite architectural detail, Tiffany-style lamps, and antique furnishings with an Afrocentric elegance is located in the historic Stuyvesant Heights District. The mansion's four guest bedrooms—the Ashante Suite, the Regal Retreat Suite, the Black Memorabilia Suite and the Jumping the Broom Suite—have their own individual style. The room rate of $100 per night (plus 8¼% sales tax) includes afternoon tea and breakfast for two. Call for more information and reservations.

TOURS OF BROOKLYN

BRAGGIN' ABOUT BROOKLYN
685 Gates Avenue
(718) 297-5107
(718) 771-0307
www.bragginaboutbrooklyn.org

This is the only company offering an African American heritage bus tour of historic Brooklyn from colonial times to the present. Stops include the Prison Ship Martyrs Monument, Bedford-Stuyvesant Restoration Corporation, Weeksville Historic Houses, Underground railroad sites, the Akwaaba Mansion, and more. Call for meeting place, schedule, and prices.

QUEENS

Map of Queens (Courtesy of Harlem Spirituals, Gospel & Jazz Tours, Inc. 212-391-0900)

4

Queens

HISTORY OF QUEENS

Queens, the largest borough, with 120 square miles, was settled by the Dutch and some English in the 1640s. As the Native Americans were forced out, the Dutch established the villages of Vlisingen (Flushing), Middleburgh (Newtown and Elmhurst), and Rustdorp (Jamaica). An English Quaker, John Bowne, was imprisoned in 1662 for holding Quaker meetings in his home in Flushing. He was subsequently banished from the colony by the Dutch West India Company. Bowne appealed the decision in the Netherlands, where the court sided with him and guaranteed religious freedom to all the colonists. Bowne returned to Flushing and became active in the abolitionist movement. The Bowne House, now a historic landmark, is across the street from the Aspinwall House Historic Site, a station on the Underground Railroad.

When the British took over the colony in 1664, they renamed this area Queens after Catherine of Braganza, the wife of King Charles II. It thrived as a farming community and was known for raising specialty crops. The first American apple, the Newton Pippin, was grown in Queens.

After the Battle of Long Island in 1776 was won by the British during the Revolutionary War, their troops occupied Queens for seven years. The troops ravaged the countryside, requisitioning crops and livestock for their own use. Queens's recovery from the pillaging and plundering was a slow process, but the building of roads in the early 1800s and the opening of the Long Island Railroad in 1836 spurred it on. Improved transportation gave the farmers a means of getting their goods to the marketplace in Manhattan. In 1848, burial grounds were banned in Manhattan because the dramatic increase in the population made real estate scarce on the tiny island, and Queens, with its wide-open spaces, became the home of several large cemeteries. The borough became known as the "borough of cemeteries."

Queens has been the site of two World's Fairs, in 1939 and 1964 in Flushing Meadows. Shea Stadium, home of the New York Mets and the New York Jets, is also in Flushing Meadows and opened in 1964. The Arthur Ashe Tennis Stadium at the U.S.T.A. National Tennis Center in Flushing is a memorial to the late tennis player, who became the first black to win the Grand Slam at the U.S. Open in 1968. Ashe also won Grand Slam titles in 1970, at the Australian Open, and in 1975, at Wimbledon.

The total population of Queens is 2,229,379. The black community, which includes a large Caribbean and African population, numbers over 446,189 according to the 2000 census information. Many black residents live in Jamaica, South Jamaica, Hollis, St. Albans, Laurelton, Cambria Heights, and Springfield Gardens. Notable African Americans who have called Queens home are musicians Louis Armstrong and Count Basie, singers James Brown and Arthur Prysock, and diplomat Ralph Bunche. The borough has evolved from a sparsely populated farm community to a multicultural urban community. The Queens of the 21st century is home to a very diverse population of Asians, Hispanics, Latinos, African Americans, West Indians, Haitians, and Africans, who live and work together in a community that continues to grow and thrive.

HISTORIC SITES AND LANDMARKS

BOWNE HOUSE
37-01 Bowne Street (between 37th and 38th Streets)
(718) 359-0528; (718) 359-0873

Built in 1661, this saltbox structure is the oldest house in Queens County. It was the home of Quaker John Bowne, an abolitionist whose successful opposition to Peter Stuyvesant, the Governor of New Amsterdam, restored religious freedom to the colony (see page 171). The Bowne House is located in Flushing across the street from the site of the Aspinwall House, a station on the Underground Railroad.

Open Tuesday, Saturday, and Sunday. Groups are admitted Monday through Friday. Admission: $2; $1 seniors and kids. Call for more information.

FRIENDS MEETING HOUSE
137-16 Northern Boulevard
(718) 358-9636

The Meeting House was the first house of worship for Quakers in Flushing. The house is still used on Sundays for religious meetings and is one of New York's oldest continuously used places of worship. It was designated a New York City Landmark and is listed on the National Register of Historic Places.

MACEDONIA AFRICAN METHODIST EPISCOPAL CHURCH
37-22 Union Street (between 37th and 38th Avenues)
(718) 353-5870

Originally founded by free blacks as the African Methodist Society in 1811, Macedonia became the third largest church in Flushing. This church, a known stop on the Underground Railroad, was used because of its close proximity to the water and its side door that led to an alley, which allowed slaves to continue their journey undetected.

THE LEWIS H. LATIMER HOUSE MUSEUM
34-41 137th Street (at Leavitt Place)
(718) 961-8585

The home of black inventor Lewis Latimer has been restored and is now a museum. The son of runaway slaves, Latimer became a draftsman and worked with Thomas Edison. Latimer invented the carbon filament in the electric light bulb. He also did the drawings for Alexander Graham Bell's first telephone.

THE LOUIS ARMSTRONG HOUSE
3456 107th Street
www.satchmo.net

This two-story house, located in Corona, was designed by architect Robert Johnson and built in 1910. Jazz musician Louis Armstrong (1901–1971) and his wife, Lucille, lived in the Corona, Queens, residence from 1943 until their deaths. Queens College is working toward opening the house, which has been designated a National Historic Place, as a museum and educational center. An annual concert series for local schoolchildren called "Pops Is Tops" takes place in the garden of the house. Children from Corona and East Elmhurst attend a live jazz concert and learn about the musical contributions of Louis Armstrong. The Armstrong Archives are currently located on the Queens College Campus in the Benjamin S. Rosenthal Library. (See sidebar, page 175.)

THE LOUIS ARMSTRONG ARCHIVES
Queens College
Benjamin S. Rosenthal Library, Room 332
65-30 Kissena Boulevard
(718) 997-3670

The Louis Armstrong Archives consist of the legendary musician's photographs, papers, scrapbooks, commercial recordings, private

LOUIS "SATCHMO" ARMSTRONG

Louis Armstrong was born in New Orleans, Louisiana, on August 4, 1901. Very poor, Louis lived with his mother and grandmother until his early teenage years, when, according to legend, he was sent to the Colored Waifs Home for shooting off a gun during a 4th of July celebration. It was while he was at the home that he learned to play the coronet.

Louis Armstrong started playing in local clubs and was taken under the wing of Joseph "King" Oliver. Playing with Fate Marable's Band, he learned to read music, and, in 1923, he joined King Oliver's Creole Jazz Band in Chicago and made his first recordings. As a young musician honing his craft, Armstrong played with the Fletcher Henderson Band and was an accompanist to blues singers Ma Rainey and Bessie Smith. His experience with the big bands enabled him to spread his wings: he began to improvise, which enhanced his extended solos. From 1925 to 1929, Armstrong made a series of recordings called the "Hot Five" and the "Hot Seven," in which he collaborated with musicians Johnny Dodds, Kid Ory, and pianist Lil Hardin, his second wife.

Louis Armstrong's musical career continued to expand. He formed his own band, appeared in Fats Waller's Broadway production *Hot Chocolate*, and the films *Pennies from Heaven* and *High Society* with Bing Crosby. He was also heard regularly on the radio.

Louis Armstrong and his band toured all over the world and he was appointed the U.S. government's Ambassador of Goodwill in 1960. Louis Armstrong lived in Corona, New York, with his wife, Lucille, from 1943 until his death in 1971. Mrs. Armstrong passed away in 1983.

The Louis Armstrong House, located at 3456 107th Street in Corona, Queens, is in the process of being made into a museum and educational center by Queens College. The Louis Armstrong Archives, which hold a vast and varied collection of Armstrong memoribilia, are housed at the Benjamin S. Rosenthal Library at Queens College. (See page 174.)

recordings, memorabilia, and musical instruments, which were discovered in his house in 1987, four years after his wife Lucille Armstrong's death. The archive mounts two exhibits a year. Past exhibits have included "Armstrong and Africa," "Breaking the Barriers: Armstrong and Civil Rights," and "Ambassador Satch: Armstrong's Role as an International Ambassador of Goodwill." The archives staff also presents a slide presentation on Louis Armstrong's legacy at schools, senior centers, and other venues. Open Monday through Friday from 10 A.M. to 5 P.M. It is best to schedule an appointment to view memorabilia.

RALPH BUNCHE HOUSE
115-125 Grosvenor Road

Built in the early part of the twentieth century, this Tudor-style house in Kew Gardens was home to African American diplomat and author Ralph Bunche from 1952 until 1971. Bunche received the 1950 Nobel Peace Prize for his work in negotiating the end of the Arab-Israeli War of 1949. As the Undersecretary General of the United Nations, Bunche continued to work for peace. The Ralph Bunche House is a private residence and is not open to the public.

QUEENS HISTORICAL SOCIETY
143-35 37th Avenue (Kingsland Homestead in Weebing Beach Park)
(718) 939-0647

The historical society, which is in Flushing, has been awarded a $25,000 grant as part of the federal initiative to identify and link Underground Railroad sites. The grant is being used to research, identify, and promote the Underground Railroad sites in the Flushing area. With the assistance of the Bowne House, the African

Methodist Episcopal Church of Flushing, and the (Queens) Quaker Meeting House, the society has begun to identify Flushing sites of the Underground Railroad. Tours of the house are available on Tuesday, Saturday, and Sunday from 2:30 P.M. to 4:30 P.M.

CULTURAL CENTERS

LANGSTON HUGHES COMMUNITY LIBRARY AND CULTURAL CENTER
The Queensborough Public Library
100-01 Northern Boulevard (between 100th and 101st
  Streets)
(718) 651-1100

This library in Corona houses New York State's largest circulating Black Heritage reading collection. The collection has over 40,000 volumes related to Black culture, with emphasis on geographic areas where Africans and African Americans have lived, including West Africa, South America, the Caribbean, Canada, and the United States. Special features of the Black Heritage Collection include the Schomburg Clipping File, the Black Newspaper Microfilm Collection, Black Magazine Microfilm Collection, and the Amistad Research Center Microfilm Collection. The library's cultural arts program hosts exhibits, film festivals, creative writing seminars and workshops, readings, discussions, concerts, and jazz brunches. Call for more information.

JAMAICA CENTER FOR ARTS AND LEARNING
161-04 Jamaica Avenue (161st Street)
(718) 658-7400

This center in Jamaica, Queens, offers art workshops and exhibits that reflect African American and urban life. Call for more information.

OTHER POINTS OF INTEREST

ARTHUR ASHE TENNIS STADIUM
U.S. Open Tennis Championships
U.S.T.A. National Tennis Center, Inc.
Flushing Meadows, Corona Park
(718) 592-0711

The stadium was named for the internationally-acclaimed tennis star, Arthur Ashe. Born in Richmond, Virginia, in 1943, Ashe was the first African American to win the U.S. Open at Forest Hills in 1968. He went on to become the first black man to win Wimbledon in 1975. An activist, author, and early opponent of apartheid in South Africa, Ashe formed with actor-singer Harry Belafonte "Artists and Athletes Against Apartheid" in 1984. Arthur Ashe died in 1993.

DINING OUT

PROPER CAFE
217-01 Linden Boulevard (at Springfield Boulevard)
(718) 341-2233

This Caribbean and soul food restaurant in Cambria Heights features specials of Corn Chowder, Jerk Chicken, Baby Back Ribs, and Curried Goat. There are also tasty Southern-style entrees of Pork Chops and Fried Chicken, as well as burgers and fries, steak, and seafood. Entertainment is also on the menu: Tuesday is Comedy Night; Wednesday, Jazz; Friday and Saturday, dancing; and Thursday and Sunday, Karaoke fanatics take to the mic.

Open seven days a week.

Richard's Place
200-05 Linden Boulevard (Farmers and Francis Lewis
   Boulevards)
(718) 723-0041

This popular Cambria Heights soul food restaurant offers traditional dishes like Fried Chicken, Barbecue Ribs, Herbed Chicken,
Smothered Pork Chops, Fried Whiting, Chicken and Waffles,
Oxtails, Stuffed Catfish, Green Beans, Macaroni and Cheese, Rice,
and Cabbage. Try the Sweet Potato Cheesecake for dessert—it's
out of this world.

Open Thursday through Saturday for dinner, and on Sunday for
brunch, lunch, and dinner. Takeout hours on Friday to Saturday
from 3:00 P.M. to 7:00 P.M., and on Sunday from Noon to 7:00 P.M.

Carmichael's Diner
117-08 Guy Brewer Boulevard
(718) 723-6908

This busy neighborhood diner in Jamaica serves up traditional soul
food such as Barbecue Ribs, Fried Chicken, and Smothered Pork
Chops. These lip-smacking main dishes are paired with sides of
Macaroni and Cheese, String Beans, Sweet Potatoes, and Cabbage.
Delicious desserts, especially the Fresh Peach Cobbler, are a must.

Open seven days a week for breakfast, lunch, and an early
dinner (closes at 7:30 P.M.).

Poor Freddie's Rib Shack
157-06 Linden Boulevard
(718) 659-7000

This well-known Jamaica take-out joint serves soul food to the
southern Queens community. The menu includes sandwiches and

dinners of Fried Chicken, Fried Fish, Pork Tips, Ham, and Pork Chops. For those who want real down-home cooking, try the Pigs Feet, Oxtails, Ham Hocks, and Hog Maws. The entrees are served with sides of Macaroni and Cheese, Coleslaw, Potato Salad, Black-Eyed Peas, Corn, and String Beans. For dessert, sample the Apple and Peach Cobbler, and the Sweet Potato Pie.

Open seven days a week for lunch and dinner. Take-out only.

J.C. RESTAURANT
112–10 Farmers Boulevard (between 111th & 113th Streets)
(718) 454-6247

Another popular take-out restaurant, J.C.'s in Jamaica specializes in seafood and serves Fried or Steamed Whiting, Catfish, Croakers, Spots, Scallops, and Shrimp. Side dishes at this Hollis joint include Potato Salad, Macaroni and Cheese, String Beans, Collard Greens, Cabbage, Yams, and French Fries. Homemade desserts such as bread pudding and cake are always on the menu.

Open Tuesday through Saturday for lunch and dinner.

SHOPPING

The Jamaica Avenue Shopping District stretches from 171st Street to Parsons Boulevard

HOUSE OF A MILLION EARRINGS
185-09 140th Avenue (Southgate and Thurston Streets)
(718) 977-0081

This shop has been in business since the 1960s, selling not only earrings but also Afrocentric paintings, handcrafted jewelry, clothing, statues, artifacts, masks, and books.

Open Monday through Saturday. Major credit cards accepted.

Jamaica Market
190-40 160th Street, 159-15 Jamaica Avenue
  (at Parsons Boulevard)
(718) 297-4708

This open-air market sells vegetables, plants, homemade foods, and handcrafted items. Open Monday through Saturday.

Anita's Gift Emporium
159-15 Jamaica Avenue (at Parsons Boulevard)
(718) 291-6733

Located inside the Jamaica Market (see above), this Afrocentric specialty shop sells figurines, ceramics, wedding favors and accessories, elegant floral arrangements, and African American greeting cards.
  Open Monday through Saturday.

D & J Bookstore
229-21B Merrick Boulevard (between 229th
  and 230th Streets)
(718) 949-5400

This bookstore stocks over 6,000 titles by and about people of color. It also boasts an extensive inventory of children's books. D & J also sells artifacts from Ghana and Nigeria.
  Open Monday through Saturday.

BRONX

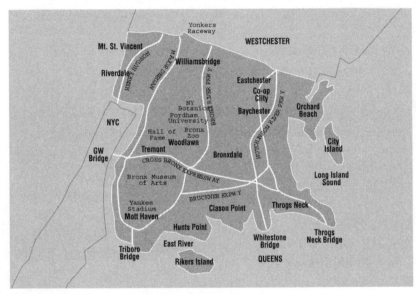

Courtesy of Harlem Spirituals, Gospel & Jazz Tours, Inc.

5

The Bronx

HISTORY OF THE BRONX

In hip-hop culture this borough is called the "boogie-down Bronx" and baseball fanatics call it the home of the Bronx Bombers. Whether it's the birthplace of rap and break dancing, or the canvas for graffiti artists' urban art, the Bronx, the northernmost borough of New York City, has a colorful history.

Originally inhabited by the Weekghasgeek Indians, this northern outpost was first settled in 1639 by Jonas Bronck, a Swedish sea captain from the Netherlands. Although settlements were destroyed in conflicts with the Weekghasgeek Indians all around him, Bronck continued to live in the area that was named for him. A short-lived peace treaty between the Indians and the Dutch was reached in 1642 at Bronck's farm (what is now 132nd Street and Lincoln Avenue). After fierce fighting between the Dutch and the Indians, and failed attempts to establish settlements near the Hutchinson River and in Throgs Neck, Thomas Pell, a physician from Connecticut, and fifteen families finally settled the eastern Bronx in 1654, naming their village Westchester. This village was the seat of Westchester County between 1683 and 1714. The Bronx remained part of Westchester County until the 1800s.

The British gained control of the Bronx in 1664 and brought with them enslaved blacks from the West Indies to work as farmhands. Documentation of the first free black in the Bronx was recorded in 1698. In the early 1700s, the borough was made up of the two towns of Westchester and Eastchester, which included the four manors of Pelham, Morrisania, Fordham, and Philipsburg.

The Revolutionary War also left its mark on the Bronx. The Battle of Pell's Point in 1776 was fought here, and the British occupied the Bronx for the remainder of the war, causing widespread destruction. The tide eventually turned, and, in 1783, General George Washington and Governor George Clinton marched from the Van Cortlandt Mansion (located in what is now Van Cortlandt Park) to take possession of New York City.

By the nineteenth century the population of the Bronx was expanding with the influx of Irish, German, and Italian immigrants. In the late 1880s the elevated trains drew even more people to the Bronx. The Bronx Botanical Garden and the Bronx Zoo opened in 1891. The Grand Concourse, a wide tree-lined avenue of apartment buildings modeled after the Champs-Élysées in Paris, was constructed in the early 1890s. The boom continued with the arrival of thousands of Yugoslavs, Armenians, and European Jews in the early 1900s. Yankee Stadium opened in 1923.

When the Great Depression hit, it halted the Bronx's rapid growth. After World War II, many of the original residents of the Bronx moved to other boroughs or to the suburbs, while displaced blacks and Hispanics moved to the south Bronx. With the construction of public housing in the south Bronx, the ethnic and economic makeup of the Bronx changed. Rent control was introduced, and housing deteriorated because of neglectful landlords. The population by the 1990s was one-third black, one-third Hispanic, and one-third Asian and white.

The fifties, sixties, seventies, and eighties were hard times for many of the residents of the Bronx, but the nineties brought signs of a turnaround. New housing construction, the opening of small businesses, a thriving Fordham Road Shopping District, and a possible renovation of Yankee Stadium are some of the positive things in the works or on the horizon for Bronx residents.

The borough is home to eleven institutions of higher learning: Fordham University, Albert Einstein College of Medicine of Yeshiva University, three colleges in the City College of New York system—Lehman, Bronx Community, and Hostos Colleges—the College of Mount St. Vincent, Mercy College, Manhattan College, the College of New Rochelle, the Maritime College of the State University of New York, and Monroe College. Often referred to as the "borough of colleges and universities," the Bronx continues to face its challenges straight on.

According to the 2000 census, the Bronx has a population of 1,332,650, of which 475,000 are black or African American. Unlike some of the other boroughs, the Bronx has few, if any, historic sites and landmarks that call attention to the history of African Americans. However, a trip to Yankee Stadium to watch the famed Bronx Bombers, the team of Bernie Williams and Derek Jeter, or a shopping trip to the Fordham Road hub are great ways to spend some time in the Bronx.

HISTORIC SITES AND CULTURAL CENTERS

VAN CORTLANDT HOUSE MUSEUM
Van Cortlandt Park
Broadway (at 246th Street)
(718) 543-3344

The mansion, built in 1748 by Frederic Van Cortlandt, a descendant of the wealthy Van Cortlandt family associated with the Dutch West India Company, is an example of plantation life in the lower Hudson Valley region. The estate was self-sufficient and prosperous, with extensive planting fields and livestock, a grist mill, and a community of craftsmen and enslaved and free field workers. George Washington used the Van Cortlandt House as his headquarters during his campaign against the British in the Revolutionary War. The museum, which is owned by the City of New York and operated by the National Society of Colonial Dames in the State of New York, is filled with furnishings and decorative arts from the Colonial and Federal periods. The museum tour includes the family's living quarters and a slave bed-chamber.

Open Tuesday through Sunday. Call for more information.

BRONX MUSEUM OF THE ARTS
1040 Grand Concourse (165th Street)
(718) 681-6000

Two small galleries in the Bronx Courthouse mix the masters with local talent, focusing on Latino and African American artists.

Open Wednesday through Sunday. Admission: $3; $2 students with ID and seniors; free for kids under 12.

BRONX RIVER ART CENTER AND GALLERY
1087 East Tremont Avenue (at West Farms Square)
(718) 589-5819
www.bronxriverart.org.

The gallery presents exhibitions of culturally and ethnically diverse themes by local, national, and international contemporary artists. The center is located in a 16,000-square-foot, four-story former warehouse. Two floors are used as artists' studio space for professionals in the rotating residency program. Bronx River Art Center offers educational programs, including free art classes for youth and adults.

Open Tuesday through Saturday. Call for more information, or visit their Web site.

MIND BUILDERS CREATIVE ARTS CENTER
3415 Olinville Avenue (at East Gun Hill Road)
(718) 652-6256

This community-based art center recently celebrated its twentieth anniversary. It offers year-round activities with a focus on African American culture, including music, dance, and theater performances. Call for a performance schedule.

SHOPPING

Fordham Road, between Jerome and Webster Avenues, is a ten-block retail paradise for young folks in search of the hippest gear. Baggy jeans, designer activewear, and the latest celebrity-endorsed sneakers are all available at this shopping mecca.

Bay Plaza Shopping Center is a sprawling shopping area right off Route 95 North on the New England Thruway. Old Navy, Modell's, Barnes and Noble, Nobody Beats the Wiz, and many other national chain stores are located here.

6

Staten Island

HISTORY OF STATEN ISLAND

Sometimes called the "borough of homes," Staten Island covers an area of sixty square miles and has a population of 443,728. Staten Island's black population is nearly 43,000, according to the 2000 census figures. Staten Island is bound by the smaller islands of Prall's Island, Island of Meadows, Hoffman Island, Swinburne Island, and Shooters Island. Staten Island is reachable from Manhattan via the famous Staten Island Ferry, which covers the five-mile stretch in twenty-five minutes. The bridges that connect Staten Island to New York and New Jersey are the Verrazano Narrows and Goethals bridges, the Outerbridge Crossing, and the Bayonne Bridge.

The Dutch colonized Staten Island in 1661 and named it Staten Eylandt after the States General, the governing body in the Netherlands. The original settlers were French Huguenots and Walloons seeking religious freedom. The ethnic makeup of Staten Island during colonial times consisted of Dutch, French Huguenots, some British, and Africans who had been brought to the colony as slaves. The settlers made their living by farming, fish-ing, shipping, milling flour, lumbering, and blacksmithing. Settlements on the shore were established around ferry landings in the eighteenth century, and licenses were granted for crossings to New Jersey, Manhattan, and Long Island, enabling farmers to take their produce to market.

During the Revolutionary War, Staten Island became a major staging point for British troops during the Battle of Long Island in August 1776. Although England won the 1776 battle, when they were finally defeated in December 1783, Staten Island became a departure point for British troops returning home.

Shortly after New York State abolished slavery in 1827, Staten Island's all-black community of Sandy Ground was established. Founded by two newly freed slaves from Manhattan, Horace K. and Silas K. Harris, the settlement was originally named Harrisville. The Harris Brothers became successful strawberry farmers and landowners.

In the 1820s Staten Island's previously successful shellfishing industry started to decline and the fishermen turned to oyster cultivation. As the island's community grew and prospered in the 1830s and 1840s, a group of free black oystermen and their families from Snow Hill, Maryland, moved to the area. The oystermen were already familiar with Sandy Ground because they had traveled up to the oyster beds in this area prior to relocating. They left their homes in Maryland to get away from repressive restrictions imposed against free blacks. In Maryland they were not allowed to assemble peacefully, possess firearms (which meant they could not hunt for food), or send their children to school. The most repressive law of 1835 required that a white person, eighteen years or older, had to be chief navigator on any boat working in the waters off the Eastern Shore. The combination of these laws made life in Maryland intolerable for free black oystermen.

At the height of its development, Sandy Ground was home to 150 black families, two schools, and two churches. One of these churches, the Rossville A.M.E. Zion Church founded in 1850, is still standing and remains the spiritual center of the Sandy Ground community.

Sandy Ground residents were active participants in the Underground Railroad. The boats of the oystermen were frequently searched for fugitive slaves traveling to Canada. The oyster industry started its decline in the early 1900s because of the pollution in the bays caused by the factories in New Jersey. When the residents of Sandy Ground could not get work in Staten Island, they sought work in New Jersey. Many of the younger residents of the community left to pursue their careers. Today, ten African American families descended from the original residents live in Sandy Ground.

HISTORIC SITES AND LANDMARKS

SANDY GROUND HISTORICAL SOCIETY, INC.
1538 Woodrow Road
(718) 317-5796

Sandy Ground Historical Society's mission is to preserve the history of the Sandy Ground community. The library and museum are open to the public. A permanent exhibit depicts the history of Sandy Ground. The changing exhibitions have featured early residents such as Joe Bishop, whose establishment of the Bishop Forge Iron Foundry was explored in "Joe Bishop—A Man & His Work." The library houses an archive called "The Black Man on Staten Island," which consists of photos, oral histories, and manuscripts documenting African American life in the borough. The library and museum present special programs, including a musical heritage series, lecture series, and an arts and crafts program for kids. Tours are also available.

The library and museum are open Saturday and Sunday. Admission: $6; $3 kids.

Rossville A.M.E. Zion Church
584 Bloomingdale Road
(718) 356-0200

The church is one of two original churches established in historic Sandy Ground. Founded in 1850 as Zion African Methodist Episcopal Church, it was and still is the spiritual center of the Sandy Ground community.

Bishop Forge Historic Site
1448 Woodrow Road

This was the site of an iron foundry established by blacksmith John Bishop in 1886. Bishop, a black man, made iron tools for the oystermen who lived in Sandy Ground. After the oyster industry died, the foundry became an integral part of construction on Staten Island and in New York City by supplying various projects with building materials. The forge was destroyed by fire in 1982.

Baymen's Houses
559, 565, and 569 Bloomingdale Road

These wooden houses are the only remaining homes of the Sandy Ground oystermen during the 1800s.

Esther V. J. Purnell Site
589 Bloomingdale Road

This was the home of Esther Purnell, an African American teacher who established one of two schools in Sandy Ground. Ms. Purnell taught adults and children at this location.

George Hunter House
575 Bloomingdale Road

George Hunter, a resident of Sandy Ground since the early 1900s, was a neighborhood treasure who became famous for his comments to a *New Yorker* magazine reporter. While on a tour of the Sandy Ground Cemetery, Hunter stated he wanted to be buried by his first wife. When asked why, it is reported that Mr. Hunter said his second wife was too strong-willed to spend eternity with. When Mr. Hunter passed away, he was buried beside his second wife.

"Pop" Pedro Site
587 Bloomingdale Road

"Pop" Pedro, the unofficial historian and mayor of Sandy Ground, lived in the community from 1881 until his death in 1988. His house was located at this site.

Isaac Harris Home
444 Bloomingdale Road

Isaac Harris was the son of Silas Harris, one of the original settlers of Sandy Ground in the 1830s. Isaac worked for the architect Stanford White, who designed some of the row houses on Striver's Row in Harlem. Legend has it that Stanford White also designed Mr. Harris's house on Sandy Ground.

7

Historic Sites Outside of New York City

WESTCHESTER COUNTY

BUSH-LYON HOMESTEAD
479 King Street (Lyon Park)
Port Chester, New York
(914) 939-8918

Constructed before the Revolutionary War, this homestead has a two-story frame slave house among its existing out-buildings. The slave quarters are not open to the public, but visitors can view the exterior of the building.

Open Thursday 1:30 P.M. to 4 P.M.

FOSTER MEMORIAL A.M.E. ZION CHURCH
90 Wildey Street
Tarrytown, New York
(914) 631-2002

Amanda and Henry Foster, Rev. Jacob Thomas, and Hiram Jimerson founded this church in 1860. Amanda Foster was born in New York in 1806. She traveled to Arkansas where she worked as a nurse for Governor Conway. While in Arkansas, Amanda started working with the Underground Railroad. She used her freedom documents to help a fugitive slavegirl escape. Amanda returned to New York and married Henry. They established their church in 1860, and the congregation worshipped at various businesses in Tarrytown until the physical church was built in 1865. During the Civil War, Foster A.M.E. Zion Church members fed and sheltered runaway slaves who were escaping to Canada.

VILLA LEWARO
67 North Broadway
Irvington-on-Hudson, New York

Hair-care entrepreneur Madame C. J. Walker built this thirty-four-room mansion overlooking the Hudson River in 1918. Designed by black architect Vertner Tandy, the same architect who designed St. Philips Episcopal Church in Harlem, the mansion cost $350,000 to construct. Madame Walker, the first black millionaire, made her fortune by inventing and selling hair-care products for black women. She employed hundreds of women in her factories and in her beauty salons. The mansion was a magnet for black leaders and entertainers of all colors. Tenor Enrico Caruso, a frequent visitor, named the house Villa Lewaro from letters in the name of Madame Walker's daughter, A'Lelia Walker Robinson. The mansion is a private residence and is not open to the public.

Front and rear views of Madame C. J. Walker's mansion in Irvington, NY (Photos by Linda Tarrant-Reid)

Harriet Tubman Underground Railroad Tour
Sisters in Support, Inc.
The Fern Tree African Gift Shop
13 South Division Street
Peekskill, New York
(914) 736-7908

The community-based Sisters in Support organizes tours to Underground Railroad sites in the northern Westchester County community of Peekskill. Located on the Hudson River, this city by the river was an obvious route for fugitive slaves on their way to freedom in Canada. Call for more information.

The following are sites on the Harriet Tubman Underground Railroad Tour:

A. G. Wells House
Main Street
Peekskill, New York

Built in the 1850s, this was the home of lawyer A. G. Wells and was a safe house for fugitive slaves on the Underground Railroad.

Park Street A.M.E. Zion Church Site
1220 Park Street
(914) 739-8830
Peekskill, New York

A stop on the Underground Railroad, this 1852 church has hidden cupboards and stairwells where fugitive slaves used to hide.

Henry Ward Beecher Site
Beach Shopping Center
Peekskill, New York

In the woods behind the shopping center is a tunnel that was once part of the land owned by Henry Ward Beecher, an abolitionist and minister of Plymouth Church. The tunnel is believed to have been a hiding place for fugitive slaves as they awaited an opportunity to flee north to Canada.

NASSAU COUNTY

AFRICAN AMERICAN MUSEUM OF NASSAU COUNTY
110 North Franklin Street (between Front Street and
   Jackson Street)
Hempstead, Long Island
(516) 572-0730

The museum has revolving exhibitions that trace the culture, history, and contributions of Africans and African Americans. Films, lectures, special events, and programs for young people complement the exhibits. The museum's educational programs for school groups include "The Struggle for Civil Rights," "African Musical Instruments," and "African Crafts." Past exhibits have included the "Role of Long Island's African Americans in the Civil War."

Open Thursday through Sunday. Call for more information.

SUFFOLK COUNTY

ST. DAVID A.M.E. ZION CHURCH
Eastville Avenue
Sag Harbor, Long Island
(631) 725-1445

Built in 1840, the church became a spiritual center for the free blacks and Native Americans who lived in the Sag Harbor area. By the early 1800s, half of the population of nearby East Hampton was composed of blacks and American Indians. The black residents were farmers, fishermen, whalers, and craftspeople. As more and more slaves made their way to Canada, St. David's became a stop on the Underground Railroad where fugitive slaves used the trap door in the pulpit to escape to freedom.

Today, Sag Harbor is home to a significant black community of writers, artists, business executives, teachers, lawyers, and retirees who are year-round and summer residents. African Americans started buying property in Sag Harbor around 1915. At that time, the waterfront property was considered less than prime real estate and was sold to blacks who established the communities of Sag Harbor Hills, Ninevah, Azure Rest, Hillcrest Heights, and Chatfields.

SAG HARBOR WHALING MUSEUM
Main Street
Sag Harbor, Long Island
(631) 725-0770

Built in 1845, this was originally the home of whaler Benjamin Huntting, and later became the summer home of Mrs. Russell Sage. The museum opened in 1936 as the Sag Harbor Historical Society, and features exhibits documenting the whaling industry in Sag Harbor. Interesting artifacts, examples of scrimshaw (carvings on whalebone), a rare gun collection, and antique children's toys are just some of the items on display at this quaint museum.

DINING OUT

NAKASAKI
276 Fulton Avenue
Hempstead, Long Island
(516) 292-9200

This innovative restaurant serves both Jamaican and Chinese dishes. Jamaican dishes include Jerk Chicken, Jerk Pork, Curry Goat, and Oxtails. Chinese dishes include *Suey Mien*—an assortment of meats atop a bed of egg noodles in chicken broth—and a Seafood Combination Platter of shrimp, lobster, scallops, and Chinese vegetables in a special sauce. On Friday and Saturday, there is Reggae, disco, house, R&B, and Calypso music on the restaurant's lower level.

Open seven days a week. Major credit cards accepted.

B. Smith's
1 Bay Street
Sag Harbor, Long Island
(631) 725-5858

This beautiful restaurant in the Hamptons offers a similar menu as its midtown Manhattan sister, with an emphasis on seafood. The restaurant is open from May through September for lunch and dinner. Major credit cards accepted. (See page 53.)

8

Calendar of Events

JANUARY

Throughout the month, there are many events honoring Dr. Martin Luther King Jr. Check newspapers, magazines, and city guides for information about these events, which take place in and around New York City.

A BROOKLYN TRIBUTE TO DR. MARTIN LUTHER KING JR.
Brooklyn Academy of Music
30 Lafayette Avenue (Ashland Place)
Brooklyn, New York

Speakers, dancers, and singers celebrate the life and legacy of civil rights activist Dr. Martin Luther King Jr. Tickets are free. For more information, call (718) 636-4100.

FEBRUARY

Programs celebrating Black History Month are offered throughout February. Check local newspapers, magazines, and other guides for events in and around New York City that focus on African American history and culture.

LANGSTON HUGHES WEEKEND
Langston Hughes Community Library and Cultural Center
Langston Hughes Library
102-09 Northern Boulevard
Queens, New York
(718) 651-6258

This weekend-long celebration of the life and works of prolific Harlem Renaissance author-poet-playwright Langston Hughes takes place the second weekend in February. Call for more information. (See page 177.)

MUSEUM FOR AFRICAN ART
593 Broadway (Houston St.)
New York, New York
(212) 966-1313

Celebrate Black History Month and the spirit of Africa at this renowned storehouse of African art and artifacts. The museum offers a series of lectures, as well as musical and dance performances. Call for more information.

NATIONAL BLACK FINE ART SHOW
Puck Building
295 Lafayette Street (Houston Street)
New York, New York
(201) 777-5218

This unique annual show features a spectacular collection of African, Caribbean, and African American paintings, sculpture, prints, photography, and fabric. Call for more information.

MARCH

MUSEUM FOR AFRICAN ART
593 Broadway (Houston Street)
New York, New York
(212) 966-1313

This Soho-based museum of African art celebrates Women's History Month with symposiums, film screenings, and special family-activity days. Call for more information.

APRIL

BLACK ROOTS FESTIVAL
Frederick Douglass Creative Arts Center
270 West 96th Street (between Broadway
   and West End Avenue)
New York, New York
(212) 864-3375

Over the years, the Frederick Douglass Creative Arts Center has featured the most talented black artists at its annual spoken-word event. Festival audiences have enjoyed readings by black poet Sonja Sanchez and writer Terry McMillan, as well as musical interludes by famous jazz musicians. Call for more information.

MAY

AFRICAN BURIAL GROUND
Elk Street (East of Broadway between Duane
   and Elk Streets)
New York, New York
(212) 432-5707

During excavation for construction of a new federal building on lower Broadway at Duane Street, workers unearthed an eighteenth-century cemetery for people of color. In May, the Office of Public Education and Interpretation of the African Burial Ground sponsors a full day of lectures, slide presentations, and tours of the historic burial ground. Call for more information.

MARTIN LUTHER KING JR. PARADE
Fifth Avenue (from 44th to 86th Streets)
New York, New York
(212) 281-9376

Formerly the 369th Regiment Armory Parade, which honored the all-black regiment called the Harlem Hellfighters who fought in World War I, the parade now celebrates both Dr. King and the black soldiers. Sponsored by the 369th Regiment Veterans Association, the parade travels from 44th Street to 86th Street along Fifth Avenue. High school and youth organization bands, unions, hospital workers, and veterans are among the participants. Call for more information.

THE PINKSTER FESTIVAL
Philipsburg Manor
Route 9-381 North Broadway (between Continental
    Street and Pierson Bellwood Avenue)
Sleepy Hollow, New York
(914) 631-3992

This celebration is an annual re-creation of the Pinkster Festival, a colonial festival observed by enslaved and free Africans and Dutch settlers in seventeenth-century New York. Under the auspices of the Historic Hudson Valley, the two-day revelry at Philipsburg Manor continues the traditions of African and Dutch dance, African storytelling, and African music played with indigenous instruments. Sign language interpreters are available if requested one week in advance. Call for more information.

Pinkster celebration, Phillipsburg Manor, Sleepy
Hollow, New York (Courtesy of Historic Hudson
Valley; photo by Tom O'Connell)

UNIVERSOUL CIRCUS
www.universoulcircus.com

Billed as "The Most Soulful Show on Earth," the Universoul
Circus is a multicultural blend of black circus performers from the
United States and around the world. To a soundtrack of classic
rhythm and blues, hip-hop, gospel, salsa, and jazz, the ringmaster,
Casual Cal, and his sidekick, Zeke, direct the action. The enter-
tainment includes everything from the death-defying high-wire act
of the Willy Family, to the unicyle basketball antics of the King
Charles Troupe. The Universoul Circus is usually in town from the
end of April through the middle of May. Check the *Amsterdam
News* or visit the Universoul Web site for more information.

JAZZ FOR YOUNG PEOPLE
Lincoln Center
33 West 60th Street
New York, New York
(212) 258-9800
(212) 258-9817
www.jazzatlincolncenter.org

Jazz at Lincoln Center presents a program for young people in May, featuring special appearances by artistic director and musician Wynton Marsalis. Call for more information.

JUNE

AN AFTERNOON OF JAZZ
Cranbury Park
Norwalk, Connecticut
(212) 290-8600

The Jackie Robinson Foundation, named for the first black baseball player in the major leagues, holds an annual fund-raiser featuring an afternoon of jazz with some of the greatest musicians and song stylists performing today. Concert-goers can kick back with a picnic lunch and enjoy the cool jazz in a beautiful, serene setting. The event takes place from noon to dusk on the last Saturday in June at Cranbury Park in Connecticut. Call for ticket information.

BLACK EXPO
Jacob K. Javits Conference Center
Eleventh Avenue (between 34th and 39th Streets)
New York, New York
(212) 234-3400

More than 300 businesses, from small independents to large corporations, gather at the Javits Center to sell goods and services of particular interest to the African American consumer. The event also features entertainment, book signings, seminars, workshops, and one-on-one discussions with African American businesspeople and representatives from major corporations. Call for more information.

BLACK FILMMAKERS FOUNDATION
670 Broadway, Suite 304
New York, New York
(212) 546-2656

The Foundation hosts an annual film festival. Call for information about scheduled screenings.

DANCEAFRICA
Brooklyn Academy of Music
30 Lafayette Avenue (Ashland Place)
Brooklyn, New York
(718) 636-4100

Since 1977, DanceAfrica has evolved from a Brooklyn-based community tradition into the largest and most prestigious festival of African and African American dance and music in the United States. The event brings together both African and U.S.-based dance troupes whose performances explore the social, religious, and ceremonial traditions of Africa. The popular DanceAfrica Bazaar is a two-day global marketplace held in BAM's parking lot, where African, Caribbean, and African American food, clothing, artifacts, jewelry, and crafts are sold. Call for more information.

JVC JAZZ FESTIVAL
New York, New York
(212) 501-1390
www.festivalproductions.net

This annual music festival features performances by major artists at venues all over New York City. In past years, attendees were treated to the music of Aretha Franklin, Ray Charles, Herbie Hancock, Cassandra Wilson, the Manhattan Transfer, Wayne Shorter, Ray Barretto, and many others. The Schomburg Center for Research in Black Culture, the Studio Museum in Harlem, Avery Fisher Hall at Lincoln Center, Carnegie Hall, and the Beacon Theater are some of the locations where devotees can hear great music. Check entertainment guides in newspapers and magazines for more information, or visit the festival's Web site.

EAST ELMHURST-CORONA FAMILY DAY
Langston Hughes Community Library and Cultural Center
Langston Hughes Library
100-01 Northern Boulevard (between 100th
   and 101st Streets)
Queens, New York
(718) 651-1100

This family-day celebration offers recreation, fun competitions, and evening concert performances for young and old. Call for more information.

JULY

THE HARLEM BOOK FAIR
West 135th Street (between Malcolm X and Adam Clayton Powell Jr. Boulevards)
New York, New York
(212) 953-3512

This annual outdoor book fair in Harlem brings together publishers, African American authors, poets, and writers to discuss, read, and sign books. Performances by spoken-word artists, musicians, and storytellers, as well as readings by authors of fiction, nonfiction, and children's books, are all part of the festivities. The all-day event is free. Call for more information.

JAZZMOBILE (JULY AND AUGUST)
(212) 866-3613
www.hometoharlem.com

The sweet sounds of jazz waft through the Big Apple on Mondays, Tuesdays, Thursday, and Fridays at various sites throughout the five boroughs. Wednesday night performances are held on the Upper West Side of Manhattan at Grant's Tomb (122nd Street and Riverside Drive). Call for more information.

RUCKER BASKETBALL TOURNAMENT
Holcombe Rucker Memorial Playground
West 156th Street (between Frederick Douglass Boulevard
  and Harlem River Drive)
New York, New York

Founded in 1950 by Holcombe Rucker to extend the winter sport into summer, the basketball tournament has been a magnet for NBA greats like Walt Frazier, Kareem Abdul Jabbar, Julius Irving, and others. Today, youth basketball teams from all over the New York City area come to Harlem to compete. The tournament is held throughout July and August, and is sponsored by corporations.

THE INTERNATIONAL AFRICAN ARTS FESTIVAL
Boys and Girls High School
1700 Fulton Street
Brooklyn, New York
(718) 638-6700

Rain or shine, this Fourth of July weekend event is extraordinary, with an extensive African marketplace where food, jewelry, artwork, clothing, and artifacts are sold. African dancers and musical acts featuring famous artists round out the program. A petting zoo and various activities for children make this an event for the entire family. Call for more information.

Recording artist Stevie Wonder at the 28th Annual International African Arts Festival's African marketplace. (Photo courtesy of International African Arts Festival)

MULTICULTURAL EXHIBITION AND SHOWCASE
Langston Hughes Community Library and Cultural Center
Langston Hughes Library
100–101 Northern Boulevard (between 100th
  and 101st Streets)
Queens, New York
(718) 651-1100

This showcase brings together the talents of the Corona, East Elmhurst, and Jackson Heights artistic communities. Held on the second Saturday in June. Call for more information.

AUGUST

HARLEM WEEK AND THE HARLEM JAZZ FESTIVAL
New York, New York
(212) 862-7200
www.discoverharlem.com

Hosted by the Greater Harlem Chamber of Commerce, this renowned celebration has expanded to become a month-long festival from August 1st to August 31st. The highlights include a street fair that stretches across West 135th Street, concerts, a film festival, fashion shows, symposiums, and sports competitions, all of which pay tribute to Harlem's past, present, and future. Call for more information.

HARLEM WEEK BLACK FILM FESTIVAL
Adam Clayton Powell Jr. State Office Building Art Gallery
163 West 125th Street, 2nd floor (at Adam Clayton
   Powell Jr. Boulevard)
New York, New York
(212) 749-5298; (212) 873-5040
www.harlem.cc.com

A two-week film festival featuring films by filmmakers of African descent. Past films presented included "Sudan on the Slave Trail," Oscar Micheaux's "Within Our Gates," and "Sankofa." Evening screenings during the week and afternoon and evening screenings on weekends. Admission: $5; $4 for students and seniors. Call for film schedule.

WEEKSVILLE SOCIETY SUMMER FAMILY FESTIVAL
1698-1708 Bergen Street (between Buffalo
   and Rochester Avenues)
Brooklyn, New York
(718) 756-5250

This annual festival for the young and the young at heart is held on the second Saturday in August. The entire family can enjoy a day of horseback riding, face painting, storytelling, and more while learning about the history of African Americans in early nineteenth-century Brooklyn. Festival vendors sell art, jewelry, and other accessories. Call for more information.

MORRIS-JUMEL MANSION MUSEUM JAZZ FESTIVAL
63 Jumel Terrace (between West 160th
  and 162nd Streets)
New York, New York
(212) 923-8008

Internationally acclaimed artists perform at "Jazz at the Mansion," an annual jazz festival. Call for more information.

CARIBBEAN CULTURAL CENTER
408 West 59th Street (between Ninth
  and Tenth Avenues)
New York, New York
(212) 307-7420

The cultural center sponsors a carnival celebrating the traditions of Afro-Caribbean and Afro-Latin cultures. Festivities include live entertainment and an African marketplace where vendors sell artifacts. The arts center also sponsors dance events at Aaron Davis Hall on the City College of New York campus at Convent Avenue and 135th Street. Call for more information.

SEPTEMBER

AFRICAN AMERICAN DAY PARADE
Adam Clayton Powell Jr. Boulevard (between 111th and
  142nd Streets)
New York, New York

This annual parade features marching bands, floats carrying local celebrities, and organizations from near and far celebrating African American culture.

DANCE THEATRE OF HARLEM AT CITY CENTER
West 55th Street (between Sixth and Seventh Avenues)
New York, New York
(212) 581-1212

One-time New York City Ballet principal dancer Arthur Mitchell wanted "to do in dance what Jackie Robinson did in baseball." When he founded the Dance Theatre of Harlem in 1969, his vision and talent transcended more than racial barriers as he nurtured previously untapped gifts in young African American dancers. The troupe's annual New York program is held in the fall. Call the City Center box office for more information.

WEST INDIAN AMERICAN DAY CARNIVAL
Eastern Parkway (between Utica and Flatbush Avenues)
Brooklyn, New York
(718) 773-4052

This Labor Day Weekend celebration is the largest annual gathering of Caribbean Americans in the United States. The festival of food, music, and dance begins with its famous parade of elaborate floats, costumed dancers, and steel drum musicians. The televised festival spans block after block on Eastern Parkway, and has become an institution where politicians, celebrities, and famous musicians make an appearance. Call for more information.

WHITNEY M. YOUNG FOOTBALL CLASSIC
Giants Stadium
Meadowlands Sports Complex
East Rutherford, New Jersey

The New York Urban League sponsors this annual face-off between two football giants from historically black colleges. For the past several years, the lineup has been Grambling University vs. Hampton University, and has featured a battle of the bands and dancers at halftime, as well. Go early and join the enormous tailgate party in the parking lot, which is like a street festival with vendors hawking T-shirts and folks selling various merchandise. For more information, call (212) 926-8000.

OCTOBER

MORRIS-JUMEL MANSION MUSEUM
65 Jumel Terrace (between West 160th
  and 162nd Streets)
New York, New York
(212) 923-8008

Celebrate Halloween at the colonial mansion that was George Washington's headquarters during the Battle of Harlem Heights. Families are invited for storytelling program for children. Call for more information.

NOVEMBER

VIVIAN ROBINSON AUDELCO RECOGNITION AWARDS
Aaron Davis Hall for the Performing Arts
City College of New York
138 Convent Avenue (West 135th Street)
New York, New York
(212) 307-7420

For more than a quarter of a century, African American luminaries—actors, directors, playwrights, producers, and designers—have been recognized for their achievements in the entertainment industry at this annual event. Call for more information.

DECEMBER

ALVIN AILEY DANCE COMPANY
City Center
West 55th Street (between Sixth and Seventh Avenues)
New York, New York

The Alvin Ailey Dance Company takes up residence at City Center for five weeks starting in December. Under the direction of former Ailey dance diva Judith Jamison, the troupe continues to perform the ever-popular "Revelations," as well as new additions to their repertoire. For information, call (212) 767-0590. For ticket information only, call City Tix at (212) 581-1212.

KWANZAA CELEBRATION
Museum of Natural History
79th Street (Central Park West)
New York, New York
(212) 769-5100

The museum's Hall of Ocean Life is converted into an African marketplace for one day of the seven-day Kwanzaa holiday, which begins on December 26th and ends January 1st. Dancers, drummers, and storytellers highlight the afternoon performances. The event is free with museum admission. Call for more information.

KWANZAA EXPO
Jacob K. Javits Conference Center
Eleventh Avenue (between 34th and 39th Streets)
New York, New York

Each year this renowned cultural event draws some 25,000 people. The four-day exposition features over 300 vendors selling art, jewelry, clothing, books, and artifacts for the holiday. International cuisine, concerts, and a fashion show also highlight the weekend. For more information, call (718) 585-3530.

CATHEDRAL OF ST. JOHN THE DIVINE
112th Street (Amsterdam Avenue)
New York, New York
(212) 662-2133

This internationally acclaimed artsy crowd's "haven" on earth hosts an ecumenical celebration at winter solstice that showcases elements of Christmas, Hanukkah, and Kwanzaa. Dancers, musicians, and singers electrify the sanctuary. Tickets are required. Call for more information.

KWANZAA CELEBRATION
Langston Hughes Community Library and Cultural Center
Langston Hughes Library
100-01 Northern Boulevard (between 100th and 101st Streets)
Queens, New York
(718) 651-1100

This one-day Kwanzaa celebration, held on the second Saturday of December, includes a crafts fair, poetry readings, and live entertainment. Call for more information.

APPENDIX A

IMPORTANT TELEPHONE NUMBERS AND WEB SITES

New York Convention & Visitors Bureau: (212) 484-1222;
www.nycvisit.com or www.newyork.citysearch.com

New York City Weather: (212) 976-1122

Greater Harlem Chamber of Commerce: (212) 862-7200

Bronx Borough President's Office: (718) 590-3500

Brooklyn Borough President's Office: (718) 802-3693

Manhattan Borough President's Office: (212) 669-8300

Queens Borough President's Office: (718) 286-3000

Staten Island Borough President's Office: (718) 816-2000

African American Association of Innkeepers International:
(877) 422-5777 or www.africanamericaninns.com

Emergency (ambulance, fire, police): 911

APPENDIX B

TRANSPORTATION INFORMATION

New York City Bus, Train, and Subway Information

General Information:	(718) 330-1234
Status Hotline (updated hourly):	(718) 243-7777
Metro Card Information:	(800) METRO CARD
	(800-638-7622)
	(212) METRO CARD
	(212-638-7622)
Reduced Fair Information:	(718) 243-4999

Mass Transit Authority Customer Service: (718) 330-3322
Mass Transit Authority Web Site   www.mta.nyc.ny.us
Westchester Metro North Trains: 1-800-METRO INFO
                                            (638-7646); (212) 532-4900;
                                            www.mta.nyc.us
Long Island Railroad: (718) 217-LIRR
                                            (718-217-5477);
                                            (516) 822-LIRR
                                            (516-822-5177)
Staten Island Railroad: (718) 966-SIRT (718-966-7478)

New York City Taxicabs

New York City Taxi & Limousine Commission (Lost Property and Complaints):
(212) 302-TAXI (212-302-8294)
www.nyc.gov/taxi

Ferry Service

Staten Island Ferry   (718) 727-2508
NY Waterway (Ferry and Bus Service):   (212) 564-8846
                                            (201) 902-8700
                                            (800) 53-FERRY

Other Information

The following are major hubs for transportation services in New York
City:

Grand Central Terminal: 42nd Street (between
                                            Lexington Avenue and
                                            Vanderbilt Place)
Pennsylvania Station: 31st to 34th Streets
                                            (between Seventh and
                                            Eighth Avenues)
Amtrak: (800) USA-RAIL
                                            (from Pennsylvania Station)
Port Authority Bus Terminal: Eighth Avenue (between
                                            40th and 42nd Streets)
                                            (212) 564-8484
                                            (201) 659-8823
                                            (212) 564-9115, TTTY/TTD

APPENDIX C

MEDIA OUTLETS

NEWSPAPERS

THE AMSTERDAM NEWS
2340 Frederick Douglass Boulevard, New York, NY;
  (212) 932-7400

This weekly newspaper covers national and local news, as well as arts and entertainment news of interest to the black community.

AFRICAN PRESS
159-19 Hillside Avenue, Queens, NY; (718) 523-6440

A monthly newspaper geared to the African community that features news from the African continent.

AFRO TIMES
1195 Atlantic Avenue, Brooklyn, NY; (718) 636-9119

A weekly paper reporting on international, national, and local news events that affect Africans, African Americans, and people from the Caribbean.

THE AFRICAN SUN TIMES
299 Broadway, Suite 716, New York, NY; (212) 791-0777

A weekly publication featuring news reports from the African continent.

The *Amsterdam News* building, on Frederick Douglass Boulevard between West 125th and West 126th Streets (Photo by Linda Tarrant-Reid)

THE BLACK STAR NEWS

P.O. Box 64, New York, NY; (212) 678-2088;
www.BlackStarNews.com

A weekly paper highlighting world and local news, it also features sections devoted to arts and entertainment, business, and health as they relate to the black community.

THE NEW YORK CARIB NEWS

15 West 39th Street, New York, NY; (212) 944-1991

Billed as "The Weekly Voice of the Caribbean-American Community," the paper reports on news from Africa, Europe, the Caribbean, and New York City.

THE FINAL CALL
734 West 79th Street, Chicago, Illinois; (773) 602-1230
www.finalcall.com

The official organ of the Nation of Islam, this weekly publication is devoted to covering the leaders, events, and programs of the Nation of Islam.

THE WEEKLY GLEANER
175-61 Hillside Avenue, Queens, NY; (718) 657-0788

This weekly newspaper serves the Caribbean American community of New York City.

THE NEW AMERICAN
1195 Atlantic Avenue, Brooklyn, NY; (718) 783-1238

A weekly newspaper featuring arts, entertainment, and sports, with an emphasis on stories of interest to the black community.

THE NEW YORK BEACON
12 E. 33rd St., New York, NY; (212) 213-8585
www.Kampung.Net/NYBeacon

Published weekly, this newspaper features world, national, and local reports, including sections on arts and entertainment and sports.

THE NEW VOICE OF NEW YORK
175-61 Hillside Avenue, Queens, NY; (718) 206-9866

The masthead bills this as "New York's Fastest Growing Interracial Newspaper!" This weekly publication covers national, local, and community news. Other sections include entertainment, education, business, and sports.

HARLEMLIVE

1330 Fifth Avenue, New York, NY; (212) 369-6275;
www.harlemlive.org

Kids from the Harlem community produce this Internet publication. Their mission is to cover events, people, and issues throughout Harlem, while learning the processes of reporting, writing,
editing, working with digital art, photography, and publishing.

RADIO

WBLS, 107.5 FM

(212) 447-1000

This is the jewel of Inner City Broadcasting's crown and one of
two minority-owned-and-operated radio stations in New York City.
This popular FM station offers a rhythm and blues format with a
steady stream of classic soul. The Top Ten is played every night
from 6 to 10 P.M.

WBAI, 99.5 FM

(212) 209-2800

The station is part of the Pacifica public radio network and provides commercial-free music, public affairs programs, political
commentary, and in-depth discussions on world and local events.

WBGO, 88.3 FM

(973) 624-8880

This New Jersey-based station plays traditional jazz. Popular programs hosted by Michael Bourne and "Jazz Maniac" Kenny Washington feature the music of jazz greats, including John Coltrane,
Duke Ellington, Horace Silver, Thelonius Monk, and Miles Davis.

WQCD, 101.9 FM
(212) 352-1010

Smooth jazz with a little rhythm and blues is on the play list of this station. African American radio personality Pat Prescott hosts a weekday morning show and a Sunday morning talk show.

WQHT, 97.1 FM
(212) 229-9797

This station, known as Hot 97, plays blazing hip-hop and R & B.

WRKS, 98.7 FM
(212) 242-9870

Rhythm and blues and classic soul dominate this popular radio station, known as Kiss FM. The syndicated "Tom Joyner Morning Show" features hit songs and free-form fun.

WLIB, 1190 AM
(212) 447-1000

The sister station to Inner City Broadcasting's WBLS-FM is now on twenty-four hours a day, and features chat programs covering community affairs, sports, health, and politics with a sprinkling of Caribbean music.

WWRL, 1600 AM
(718) 335-1600

This rhythm and blues station plays 100% pure soul and classic oldies. On Sundays, Gospel programs dominate the lineup.

SUGGESTED READING

The Autobiography of An Ex-Colored Man by James Weldon Johnson. A. A. Knopf, New York, 1927.

The Best of Simple by Langston Hughes. Hill and Wang, New York, 1997.

The Big Sea by Langston Hughes. A. A. Knopf, New York and London, 1940.

The City of Refuge: The Collected Stories of Rudolph Fisher edited by John McCluskey Jr. University of Missouri Press, Missouri, 1987.

Five Plays by Langston Hughes edited by Webster Smalley. Indiana University Press, Indiana, 1968.

Harlem: Negro Metropolis by Claude McKay. E.P. Dutton & Co., New York, 1940.

Harlem Shadows by Claude McKay. Harcourt Brace and Co., New York, 1922.

Home to Harlem by Claude McKay. Harper, New York, 1928.

Lush Life, A Biography of Billy Strayhorn by David Hajdu. Farrar Straus Giroux, New York, 1996.

Music Is My Mistress by Duke Ellington. Doubleday & Co., Inc., New York, 1973.

The New Negro by Alain Locke. A and C Boni, New York, 1925.

Plum Bun: A Novel With a Moral by Jessie Redmon Fauset. Frederick A. Stokes Company, New York, 1928.

Short Stories, Langston Hughes edited by Akiba Sullivan Harper. Hill and Wang, New York, 1996.

The Souls of Black Folk by W. E. B. DuBois. Dodd, Mead, New York, 1961.

Their Eyes Were Watching God by Zora Neale Hurston. Negro Universities Press, New York, 1937.

The Weary Blues by Langston Hughes 1926.

FOR KIDS

Black Americans of Achievement Series by Chelsea House Publishers, New York. A series of biographies about African Americans including Ralph Abernathy, Muhammad Ali, Louis Armstrong, Arthur Ashe, Ella Fitzgerald, Thurgood Marshall, Charlie Parker, Walter White, Paul Robeson, James Weldon Johnson, Harriet Tubman, and many others.

SOURCES

Black Legacy: A History of New York's African Americans by William Loren Katz.

Colonial New York—A History by Michael Kammen. KTO Press, 1975.

Cotton Club by Jim Haskins. New American Library, 1977.

The Encyclopedia of New York City edited by Kenneth Jackson. Yale University Press, 1995.

Harlem: The Making of a Ghetto, Negro New York, 1890–1930 by Gilbert Osofsky. HarperCollins, 1966.

Harlem On My Mind: 1900–1968 edited by Allen Schoener. Random House, 1968.

Harlem Today, A Cultural and Visitors Guide by A. Peter Bailey and Edith J. Slade. Gumbs & Thomas Publishers, Inc., 1994.

Hippocrene U.S.A. Guide to Black New York by Joann Biondi and James Haskins. Hippocrene Books, Inc., 1994.

A Negro History Tour of Manhattan by M. A. (Spike) Harris. Greenwood Publishing Corp., 1968.

The Norton Anthology, African American Literature, general editors, Henry Louis Gates, Jr. and Nellie Y. McKay. W.W. Norton & Company, Inc., 1997.

The Sound of Harlem (album) produced by Frank Driggs, Jazz Odyssey, Vol. II. Text by George Hoefer.

This Was Harlem: A Cultural Portrait, 1900–1950 by Jervis Anderson. Farrar, Straus and Giroux, 1982.

Touring Historic Harlem, Four Walks in Northern Manhattan by Andrew S. Dolkart and Gretchen S. Sorin. The New York Landmarks Conservancy, 1997.

When Harlem Was in Vogue by David Levering Lewis. Oxford University Press, 1981.

INDEX